X

DISCARD

Peter Richmond

Simon & Schuster

My Father's War

A Son's Journey

-M- 7|96 23.00

SIMON & SCHUSTER
Rockefeller Center
1230 Avenue of the Americas
New York, NY 10020

SIMON & SCHUSTER and colophon are registered trademarks
of Simon & Schuster Inc.

Designed by Deirdre C. Amthor

Manufactured in the United States of America

10 9 8 7 6 5 4 3 2

Library of Congress Cataloging-in-Publication Data is available.

ISBN 0-684-80040-3

To Maxfield and Hillary

Contents

Acknowledgments 9

PART I: Guadalcanal 13
PART II: New Britain 81
PART III: Peleliu 167

Acknowledgments

Jeff Neuman at Simon & Schuster stood behind this book where few others would have, and then guided its creation with an editing expertise of which few others—as any of his writers will attest—are capable. David Granger at GQ, under whom I continue to serve the best apparent apprenticeship in magazine journalism available in the land, edited the original GQ story in characteristically demanding fashion. Art Cooper, GQ's editor-in-chief, who has made a career of (among other things) nurturing, cajoling, inspiring, and encouraging writers, supported this project with the same whole-hearted enthusiasm he has shown in my five years on his staff. I have been extraordinarily privileged to work with all three; they are any writer's dream come true.

I cannot thank every marine who helped in the research

of this book. There are too many. But it was George Mac-Gillivary at the U.S. Marine Corps Historical Center who opened the first doors onto my father's world and helped me every step of the way. Vincent Brennan of the First Marine Division Association was instrumental in not only leading me to my father's men but in convincing me that this project was worth pursuing. I also want to thank Al Decker of the association, and Barbara Krieper at the Dartmouth Library.

In addition, given the rare opportunity to do so, I'd like to thank the people who taught me to do what I do—in chronological order: Tom Yankus, David Milch, the late John Hersey, Tom McCormack, Eve Zibart, Henry Allen, Bob Wright, Melissa Davis, Gene Weingarten, Al Tays, Janet Chan, and Robert Vare—as well as Esther Newberg at ICM, who has been willing from the start to back me up, and believe in the work.

A final crucial note: I am not a military historian, and this book is not intended to be a definitive account of any of the battles. One of my father's men, recounting a battle on Peleliu, paused in a conversation to caution me: if another man who had been in the same foxhole as he were to recount the same battle, the details would be entirely different. This work is intended to be a memoir. While I've tried to be as diligent as possible in reconstructing the battles of Guadalcanal, New Britain, and Peleliu, my research has reinforced the subjective nature of written history; even texts considered definitive proved to be at variance with each other. Readers looking for pure history will find titles cited in the book worth pursuing. In the meantime, anyone looking for first-person accounts of which there are no equal should seek out Richard Tregaskis's *Guadalcanal Diary*; William Manchester's *Goodbye, Darkness*; and—above all—Robert Leckie's *Helmet for My Pillow*.

PART I
Guadalcanal

I KICK THE HAND GRENADE without thinking. My brain shouts out in panic, but it is too late; I've already punched it with the toe of my boot, and as soon as I see that the pin is missing, fear begins to blossom inside me. Somehow, under the blood-rush of my adrenaline, a quiet corner of my brain takes note of the surprising weight of it, the crunching sound it makes as it rolls across the bone-dry dirt, turning over four or five or six times, just long enough for me to imagine shrapnel fanning out in an arc and stitching its way across my waist, or my thighs, or my face.

Then it stops rolling. It does not explode.

I want to blame my foolishness on sunbaked stupor. The August midday equatorial sun has bleached all the color from a cloudless sky and the heat is a tangible thing; it clamps down on the field of kunai grass like a fog I can't see. But I know there is something else responsible: I've kicked an American hand grenade on Guadalcanal, on

15

Edson's Ridge—Bloody Ridge in Marine Corps lore, the pivotal battle of the pivotal campaign of World War II—because, for a single moment, my lust for my father's war has blotted out my reason.

"Through two nights, all hell broke loose," one of my father's lieutenants told me about the ridge. "And after that thing was over, some kid who had been through all of that, he said, 'Oh—here's a grenade, I'm going to move it so nobody kicks it accidentally.'

"With that we all screamed at him, and it went off and killed him. He survived two days of hell, and he tried to do a good thing, and he died."

It occurred to me that, while the odds were long, the hand grenade at my feet might have been thrown by my father, the twenty-six-year-old captain and commander of G Company, Second Battalion, Fifth Marine Regiment, First Marine Division. He'd lost thirty men on this ridge as he'd darted up and down the line, shouting orders, rushing to the breaches himself, while the Japanese stormed the hill in the middle of the night from below. He'd come up at four in the morning, at the height of the fighting, because the commander of the division had deemed the ridge to be essential, and Tom Richmond's company to be the best company available.

Or perhaps the tin drinking cup was his. In this patch of field fifty yards off a dirt road, cleared by a recent brush-fire, the cup seemed out of place amid the detritus of war I'd found: the shock-absorber spring of a Japanese artillery piece; yards of barbed wire; a shell from a .50-caliber machine gun—a misfired round, the brass edges jagged and sharp. I wondered whether, in the heat of the battle, when

16

the fighting had become hand-to-hand, a marine had hurled his drinking cup to repel a bayonet charge. Or had reached for a grenade in the chaos, in the darkness, and thrown his drinking cup instead.

The cup was lying next to half of a Japanese boot—the top half, the leather with the eyelets in it. The bottom half of the boot was nowhere to be seen. The edges of the leather were ragged and torn away. None of the forces I was acquainted with could have ripped leather like this, as if it were paper.

After I saw the boot, I didn't look any farther. I put the shell in my pocket and walked out of the field, stopping for a moment to pull out from beneath my shirt a spider the size of a silver dollar. I was numb, I guess, and too exhausted even to recoil at its size; I tossed it at my feet and it skittered away on the caked dirt road.

I thought about the balance, the symmetry of it all had the grenade gone off: for me to die on Edson's Ridge, on Guadalcanal, where half a century earlier my father prayed every night that it would be he, and not another of his young lieutenants or sergeants or corporals, who would be the one killed in battle the next day.

His prayers went unanswered. He survived Guadalcanal, and New Britain, and Peleliu, and came home in 1945 to work in the family business, manufacturing paper bags in a brick factory next to the railroad tracks in Long Island City, an industrial enclave just across the East River from midtown Manhattan.

He married the woman who would become my mother and moved to the town of Bronxville, in Westchester County, just north of New York City, to raise three children, join the country club, and go about the business of life in Eisenhower America—until December 16, 1960, when he was scheduled to return in the evening from a business trip to Chicago. He had finished up early in order to make it home in time for a scout meeting back in Bronxville, where he was a scout leader. He caught an earlier flight.

Late that morning, in rain and snow over Staten Island, my father's plane, a United DC-8 en route to Idlewild (now Kennedy) Airport, collided in midair with a TWA Super Constellation en route to LaGuardia. The TWA plane fell immediately. The United jet stayed in the air for eight miles as the pilot tried to reach Prospect Park in Brooklyn. He came up short and the jet crashed in the Park Slope section of Brooklyn, landing on a church and breaking up on Seventh Avenue.

My father was forty-four years old when he died. The Marine Corps wanted to give him a full ceremonial burial at Arlington Cemetery, with a twenty-one-gun salute. My mother decided she wouldn't be able to endure the ceremony; she did not want to hear the gunfire, she told me several years later.

I was seven at the time of the accident, so I never had a chance to ask my father about his war, but as I grew up it was always there, stored in the trunk that sat in the darkest corner of the cellar: a Japanese flag, stained with Rorschach blotches of blood, the orange circle still bright, the field of white crowded with the Japanese characters that identified the man whose blood had graced it.

I spent a lot of time with the flag, running it through my hands, marveling at the liquid feel of the silk, at how its texture differed from the rest of my father's mementos: the Japanese machine gun, the Japanese hand grenade, the rifles—all of them so inconceivably heavy and redolent of good grease and iron that I knew they carried the real weight of war.

I knew that there was horror involved in what he'd seen and done, because tucked into the trunk along with a box of medals, a sword, and his blue dress uniform was a copy of the June 6, 1944, *Life* magazine whose cover was the reproduction of a painting by a man named Tom Lea. It depicted a marine who had just landed on Peleliu. Half of his face was missing, his left arm hung at his side, and gruesome, bloody fibers were painted where his forearm and hand had once been. The illustration was fascinating to me in the way that the Civil War trading cards that came out just about the same time were fascinating, but where I could look at the Civil War cards, with their bloody illustrations, the way any little kid looks at scary things, I could not look for long at the *Life* cover. I don't think I ever even looked inside to see the rest of Lea's illustrations.

The trunk contained the commonplace reminders of his tour of duty; the real prize he kept at the family's farm in the Berkshire Hills of Massachusetts: the bomb carrier, a military truck painted green. Straw leaked through the cracked leather of the seat, and its gearshift was a long shaft of iron, the knob hard and black. The truck's bed was outfitted with a hoist to lift ordnance. In the winter, when the roads were impassable, he'd park our station wagon out near the highway, leaving us huddled in the cocoon of the heated company Chrysler, and disappear into the darkness on foot, returning to ferry us in to the farm aboard the bomb carrier.

I don't know why we called it the farm; its only crops were goldenrod and pine trees, one thousand acres of them. He bought the place right after the war. The house was equipped with neither plumbing nor electricity, and he never added either. I think the farm served as a counterbalance to his life in Westchester and Long Island City. I know he needed one. In another *Life* magazine, published in December 1957, the editors devoted a dozen pages to an examination of the cocktail party; in one of the photographs my parents are shown, mingling, in a Cheevered living room. My mother is smiling at another guest, perfectly at home. My father stands in the back of the room, grim-faced.

He didn't like the parties. My mother used to tell him about this party or that party they'd been invited to; parties were the current on which my hometown floated. Have a good time, he'd tell her. Have someone take you. I'm going to the farm that weekend.

He loved the farm. The farm had the two things that made him happiest in his life: wilderness and snakes. He'd spend every weekend, every vacation, out in that forest, cutting down pines with a yellow chain saw and planting new ones. I suppose that was the balance of his life's equation; during the week, he turned trees into paper bags, and during the weekend he planted the new trees.

I knew my father by the whine of his chain saw. At the end of the day he'd come out of the woods, fit and compact, muscular, the sweat thundering out of him, carrying a milk snake, or a garter, or even a king. Later he'd sit on the porch next to my mother, gazing down at his lake. I'd sit in front of him, my legs dangling over the edge of the porch, over the dark space where the porcupines lived, and listen to the laughter of the ice in his glass of bourbon. I don't remember him saying a great deal; I remember the sound of my mother's voice, but I don't remember my father's.

Sometimes he'd take me up to the farm in the dead of winter alone, late on a Friday night. He drove very, very fast—his Chryslers were always ordered from the factory, with the largest street-legal engines; my mother recalls being reduced to tears at the speed of his driving, and begging him to slow down, and his not responding, just driving on, faster. I'd sit on the front seat next to him, beneath the blast of the heater and the green-blue glow of the dashboard. I was too small to see out the windshield, but I could feel the speed of the car in the way it would hit the bumps in the Taconic Parkway and seem to go airborne for a second before settling back with a bounce of the shocks. The rhythm of the bouncing would lull me; his right thigh was my pillow. I'd wake up as we bumped down the last few miles of dirt road, and he'd carry me over his shoulder through the dark, frozen farmhouse, the floorboards squealing, and tuck me into a crib beneath piles of quilts. I remember the absolute blue of the cold, and a starscape in the blackness out the window. I'd fall back asleep to the sound of the first crackles of the fire he'd set in the woodstove downstairs.

Sometimes he'd shoot the rifles he'd brought back from the Pacific. The barrel of the machine gun had been filled with lead, but the rifles worked. One was a Japanese infantry rifle; I remember stroking its wooden stock. The bullets for all of them were huge. I was never allowed to shoot any of them, but I would watch him—the blue flame leaping from the barrel, the concussion shocking the winter air, the sound louder than anything I'd ever heard, echoing again and again and again as it bounced off the hills and the snow, muffled by the pines. The empty kerosene cans he used as targets would fly up into the air and land a few yards away, and the holes in them were jagged and tortured.

At home, in Bronxville, where he had no forest to which he could retire, he'd retreat to the cellar, where he kept an enormous and elaborate model-train layout complete with dozens of tracks, and towns, and mountains. It spanned the breadth of the cellar, and four holes had been sawed into the table/landscape. I could crawl under it and stick my head up through them and see different parts of the scale-model world. I was barely tall enough to see the trains; I remember the scent of the puff-smoke pellets he'd put in the locomotive smokestacks, and the burnt-ozone smell of all of the electricity, and the sight of him standing at his enormous transformer, watching the half-dozen trains going around, winding their way in and out of the tunnels, making their circuits over and over again. Just watching them.

The only thing his daily life back in Westchester offered to remind him of his days in the military was the Boy Scouts, and he took it seriously. My oldest brother, who was in my father's scout pack, remembers the complexity of their marching formations, and the severity of my father's parade-ground drills; when they marched in the local parades, my father's scouts were never out of step.

I think that he was a simple man living a quiet life, and would have gone on being one until his death—a typical man in a sensible time, uncelebrated and competent, one brick in a wall. He had three children, some debt, two cars, a suburban house, and a management job in manufacturing. He may have been happy, he may not have been; it's possible that the question never occurred to him. He liked the opera. He was active in scouting. He was a good and happy drinker in a time of good and happy drinking, and by all accounts faithful to his wife and uncomplaining in his daily strife. In my father's time, for members of the business/merchant class, the amount of work you put into something was exactly commensurate with the reward you reaped, and I think he was lucky to have had that certainty about things.

The other certainty he had about himself, the other foundation of his life, was not a matter of luck. It derived from his going to war, and doing in combat what was expected of him, and perhaps a little more than was expected, so that for the rest of his life he could know that he had taken the most essential test a man can take in life, and passed it. And that is as certain a certainty as any man has ever known—ever since man, and ever since war, which are nearly the same length of time.

It took no special courage or backbone for him to enlist in the armed forces in peacetime. His best friends all did the same thing. In 1936, when my father enlisted while a sophomore at Dartmouth College, there were fewer political issues attached to the military arm of the nation, not the way it would be by the time we got to Vietnam, when politicians took over the warfare. In 1936 the relationship between the civilian and the military was still a lot like it had been at the nation's inception, when General George Washington resigned his commission as soon as he'd won the Revolutionary War: the military served the people when they needed it to, and then it was put away until it was needed again, and when it was needed again, there would be men ready to go—the right balance, I think.

When my father and his friends joined the armed forces, it was because it was a routine thing to do. And part of the reason it was routine was that the military was not yet perceived as something to be used largely for political purposes.

As for his joining the Marine Corps as opposed to any other branch, this was a slightly different matter. Of the armed services, the Navy was the most fashionable and patriotic, and to be a marine within the Navy was to be something of an elite warrior. They were traditionally the first to land and the last to leave. Their dress uniforms were snappy as hell.

Once the war broke out, and they had to fight, nothing special was required of my father's character for him to endure the training, get in the boats, and land on the beaches; there wasn't a great deal of choice. Going over the hill was shame enough for a lifetime, because the cause you were deserting was a noble one. Circumstances of the time made it impossible not to go along with it. Maybe impossible not to want to lead. What forged the man, and his generation, was the ability to blot out the fear, and to subsume his individual life for the life of the larger good.

One of my father's men would later tell me that the first thing my father said to the men around him in their first foxhole in Guadalcanal was, "There's only one direction to face in this hole: toward the enemy." The choice had been made, irrevocably and certainly. That it was a choice that most everyone made, and that four years later it proved to have been the right one, made it mundane to the men who made it.

A half century later, though, I can't ignore its magnificence. The power of that sense of duty is reflected in a letter I found in a file in the marine archives in Washington, D.C. It was written to one of my father's fellow officers by a corporal named John King on the eve of the First Marine Division's departure from Parris Island for the South Pacific.

"Dear Sir," it begins, in careful script:

I realize the request I am about to make is most unusual and therefore will seem strange to you, but if this be the case, I hope you will not look upon it with disfavor when you view my case. Last night I received word that I have been scheduled to be transferred out of this regiment, for duty with a training battalion. Now sir, I realize that the Fifth is on the verge of departing for duty that may bring it into action against the enemy. To leave the regiment which I have served with such pride is really a shattering blow to one who was so proud to be one of its members, and had hoped to see action with it when the time came. Frankly, sir, I love the old outfit, and pray that you remove my name from the Transfer list and let me go with you. I realize that the road ahead is not an easy one, and being a marine, I never have expected it to be. Being twenty-one years of age, with no one depending upon me for support, and being ready, willing and able, I can think of nothing I'd rather do than "shove off" with the outfit I have been through so much with. Since I have been in the Marine Corps I have done my best to live up to its traditions. My record book is free from blemishes caused by misconduct, and honestly, sir, I have tried to be worthy of my

uniform. To be sure, I haven't been faultless, but how many of us are? Now that the occasion has arisen where I must make this request of you, I hope that you will find it possible to grant this appeal for me. I beg your kind consideration of my case, and will be ever grateful if you can help me stay with my regiment. Thanking you in advance for any thing you might be able to do
   I remain,
    Yours sincerely,
     Corporal John T. King.

I'm still not sure why so many years passed before I grew curious about my father's war. It's possible, I guess, that I was afraid that if I did some research and asked some questions, I'd discover that he hadn't been the hero that every kid wants his dad to be. More likely, I think, was something like the opposite explanation: that part of me didn't want to know how brave and fearless a soldier he'd been. I'd have gone to Canada if I'd been drafted during Vietnam—if I'd drawn a lower lottery number—and maybe I feared that if I ever found out I was the son of a true war hero I would be ashamed of myself.

But now I'd reached an age when my own mortality was obvious; my son had passed the age of seven years and eight months, so he'd had a father longer than I had. In a sense, I was now expendable; I'd managed to grow up relatively normal without a father, and why shouldn't he be able to? And I had begun to sense that if I were to die knowing nothing about the battles, the truth and horror and beauty of Guadalcanal, New Britain, and Peleliu would have been lost to two generations: mine and my son's.

On another level, I suppose, I was seeking out my father's help. I wanted to ask him how to be a father to my son, since I had no example to follow, and if I couldn't ask my father in person, at least I could enlist the help of his example, his legacy.

" 'By their deeds they serve'—that was your father," one of his men would tell me some time later. If it were true—and I would come to learn that it was—then knowing his deeds would be nearly as good as talking with the man himself.

I decided to go to the South Pacific to find, as best I could, those parts of his war that could still be touched and felt, that could be as tangible to me as the silk of his Japanese flag. I set out, two months after my fortieth birthday, to find pieces of the war as a way of finding pieces of him.

I pored through the histories for mention of my father's name. There was nothing in Richard Tregaskis's fine work of war correspondence, *Guadalcanal Diary,* the most popular account of the battle. Nothing in John Hersey's *Into the Valley,* which chronicled the exploits of Captain Charlie Rigaud's company in Guadalcanal. Nothing in *Helmet for My Pillow,* Robert Leckie's lively First Regiment memoir. Nothing in Eric Hammel's *Starvation Island* or in the most recent and comprehensive tome, Richard Frank's *Guadalcanal.*

I had not yet figured out exactly why it was so difficult to find literary reference to my father, while countless other soldiers, many in his command, were cited with frequency: because, for the last thirty-five years, he hadn't been alive to be interviewed.

I was surprised at the number of books written about Guadalcanal; it wasn't until I read William Manchester's moving memoir, *Goodbye, Darkness*—again, no mention of Tom Richmond—that I began to understand why history was so concerned with Guadalcanal. Michener compared it to Valley Forge and Shiloh.

"Over the millennia of war," Manchester writes, "certain crack troops must be set apart, elite units which demonstrated gallantry in the face of overwhelming odds. There were the Greeks and Persians at Thermopylae, Xenophon's Ten Thousand, the Bowmen of Agincourt, the Spanish Tercios, the French Foreign Legion of Camerone, the Old Contemptibles of 1914, the Brigade of Guards at Dunkirk.

"And there was the olio of leatherneck units who fought on the Canal under the name of the First Marine Division."

In less eloquent language, Herman Wouk wrote of Guadalcanal, "It was, and remains, 'That fucking island.' "

Most of the books share one thing: the refrain that is now legend, quoting the veteran of the Canal as he reports to the afterlife:

And when he gets to Heaven, to St. Peter he will tell,
"One more marine reporting, sir. I've served my time
in hell."

I obtained a copy of his service records from the National Personnel Records Center in St. Louis. The records showed that in August of 1942 my father landed on Tulagi, and on Guadalcanal two weeks later. The papers told me that he fought on Guadalcanal for six months, that he went with the rest of the division to Australia to recuperate for ten months, and that he was in the hospital for half of that time. In December 1943 he landed on the island of New Britain, in New Guinea, and left four months later. In September of 1944 he landed on the island of Peleliu, in the Palau chain, and left two months later. In January of 1945 he came home. Those were the facts as recorded by the marine command.

My mother could remember the name of only one person with whom he had fought: Harry Connor, his classmate at Dartmouth, class of '38. I tracked Connor down, but he had passed away.

I went to Washington, D.C., to the Marine Corps Historical Center, located in the Navy Yard on the banks of the Anacostia River. On the third floor, on the main wall I saw a giant full-color reproduction of the blue-diamond First Division patch. I was staring at it when a young marine said to me, "Guadalcanal," nodding at the poster.

"I know," I said.

"It's yours for fifty bucks," he said, laughing.

"No thanks," I said. "I already have a real one."

In the archives behind the library, I found a man named George MacGillivary, a wiry, white-haired gentleman, himself a Guadalcanal vet, who told me that his archives contained a box of letters from several Guadalcanal veterans who'd written Eric Hammel to help Hammel in the research for his book a decade ago. I said I'd like to see them.

MacGillivary disappeared into the back of the archives room, and returned with a cardboard box. He said he could find only a couple of letters from men in my father's battalion, which comprised a thousand men.

MacGillivary pulled a file out of the box.

"Did your father know a Harry Connor?" he asked.

"Yes," I said.

I reached into the file, pulled out an envelope and took a letter from it, and began to read the first page I'd pulled out. "Dear Eric," read Harry Connor's letter to Eric Hammel. "Your first letter says you need to develop some characters. I don't know how successful I can be along this line as we are going back a lot of years, but as I was in the Fifth Marines for 44 months it is true I served with and for several people who enjoyed a lot of 'print' because skilled writers like John Hersey, who wrote 'Into The Valley'— mainly about Charlie Rigaud—realized as you have that they had to have a character that would appeal to their readers. The American public had and still has a great thirst for heroes. I must tell you I was quite cynical about this type of authorship. If you read 'Into the Valley' carefully, you would get the impression that H Company was leading the attack toward the Matanikau. It never happened like this; both Tom Richmond and I had our companies out front."

Seeing my father's name on the first page of the first letter, I should have been struck by the magnitude of the coincidence, but I wasn't—I was too busy hurtling through Harry Connor's papers.

The letters made several references to my father, including Harry's remembrance of the day that the two of them, as undergraduates at Dartmouth, had answered an ad in the campus paper to join the ROTC program.

His letters also included maps of the island of Guadalcanal, dates of battles, names of soldiers they'd fought with, and voluminous excerpts from his combat diary.

I had found a goldmine, and it was overwhelming. I'd hoped, at best, for a glimpse. Instead I'd been handed a window onto the war. And more: Harry's letters pinpointed the exact places on the island where my father had set foot.

I called Harry Connor's widow to tell her I was going to Guadalcanal. I told her I was going to write about it, and asked her permission to use her husband's letters. She said that Harry would have been honored. I told her that I didn't know what I was looking for but that I felt a pull. She said she understood.

Then she said, "Lift a toast to my Harry when you're over there."

I told her I would.

By the spring of 1942, Japanese forces controlled a million square miles of land and sea, nearly one-seventh of the globe, but no one felt the need to commit American ground forces to the war in the Pacific until a reconnaissance plane, flying over the Japanese-held Solomon Islands, confirmed reports that an airfield was near completion on an island called Guadalcanal, a few hundred miles north of Australia. The reports had come from a band of coast-watchers—Australians who remained on the island after the Japanese invaded the Solomons, living in the hills and watching the Japanese troop movements.

So in May of 1942 the First Marine Division left Norfolk, Virginia, to engage a Japanese force that outnumbered them by three to one. The First Marine Division was the logical choice for the job. The ground-soldiering branch of the Navy, the Marine Corps was the only branch of the armed services made up entirely of enlisted men— men who had volunteered their lives for war.

The First Marine Division was nearly 10,000 men strong, divided into three regiments. Its commanders would have told you at the time that they were the best soldiers the United States had to offer, and they would have been telling the truth.

Technically, the marines are supposed to land some-where, capture the objective, and then let the Army take over. It seldom worked that way in the Pacific war. In the Pacific, as a rule, the marines landed, captured places, slaughtered Japanese, were slaughtered themselves, grew sick, grew hungry, rotted, went nuts, won the island, and then let the Army come in—whereupon, on occasion (on Peleliu, for example), the Army would give some of it back to the Japanese, and the marines would have to return to the front to take it back again.

My father was on a converted cruise ship, the SS *America* —now the USS *Wakefield*—and joined the division in an Australian army camp forty miles from Wellington. After training exercises at Fiji, the division left Wellington in May for an unknown destination. The division still had not been apprised of the plan, which was to invade the Solomon Islands in August, in a two-pronged assault: the bulk of the division would land on Guadalcanal, with the intent of seizing the airfield. Simultaneously, the First Raider Battalion, the elite battalion of the division, under the command of the legendary Colonel Merritt Edson, would land on Tulagi, an island twenty miles to the north, where the Japanese headquarters were located, and where the capital of the British Solomon Islands had been before the Japanese took the Solomons in the 1930s.

Edson's battalion, it was decided, needed another battal-ion to support it. General Alexander Archer Vandegrift, the commander of the First Division, decided that the most battle-ready troops in the division were the four companies

—E, F, G and H—of the Second Battalion. My father was the commander of G company—the G-2-5.

Edson's men cut across Tulagi; the 2-5 came up the south side, through an abandoned cricket field. My father's company was to clean out Japanese troops from the caves that Edson's men had missed. The Japanese had stuffed themselves into them, knowing they'd never get out alive. Bish Doherty remembers Tulagi. Bish was a lieutenant in G-2-5. He remembers one cave in particular.

"We laid flame into it," he told me. "Your father and I went in. We stepped on ten or fifteen bodies. You could hear them."

They weren't dead?

"Well, they were dying."

I discovered the details of another assault my father engineered on a cave on Tulagi in a story from January 1943 in a Cleveland newspaper. Ralph C. Frey, a marine lieutenant in my father's company, recuperating at home from wounds he had received on Guadalcanal, was being written about by his hometown paper. The story quoted from a running account of one operation on Tulagi:

> Toward the end of the day, while the marines were deploying about, wondering what to try next, eight Japs dashed out, firing as they came. Key riflemen placed to cover the cave's mouth picked them off. The marines thought the cave was empty, and Frey started to enter. He was met by another barrage of Japs.
>
> When darkness fell the marines stretched barbed wire in a semicircle around the cave's entrance and attached tin cans to the wire, so the cans would rattle in case the Japs tried to escape during the night.
>
> "About 3 in the morning," Frey continued, "we

heard the cans rattling and my sentry picked off another Jap. That made nine, but shots still came from the inside every time we got in front of the entrance."

The next day and night passed in about the same manner. Several charges of TNT were thrown in and shook the ground with their explosions—but still Jap bullets came from the cave.

On the morning of the third day, another officer, Capt. Tom Richmond, a Dartmouth graduate from Yonkers, N.Y., joined Frey.

Since Frey was a lieutenant, and my father a captain and the commanding officer of the company, this meant the battalion commander had brought my father in to take command of the operation.

Richmond had some mortar shells, and by connecting several of these shells with all the TNT they had left, the marines improvised an awkward but powerful charge.

"We sneaked right up to the mouth of the cave, timed the charge to explode immediately after it left our hands and heaved it in," Frey related. "Then we ran like hell.

"The explosion knocked us on our faces, blew the entire top and side off the cave and scattered Jap bodies all about. We went back to count them and, to our amazement, found 28 dead Japs! That made 37 who had been in the cave for two days and two nights. It wasn't a big cave, and they must have been piled on top of one another four deep.

"Several, we found by examining the bodies, had

committed hari-kari. I think half of them must have been dead before the final explosion got the rest."

A man named Ray Fenton, who fought with my father, later told me something that reminded me of the cave on Tulagi. "I used to think the Marine Corps theory was that we may do it wrong, but if we all do it together, we may get away with it," he said. "By sheer force of energy and determination we did things that realistically shouldn't have been attempted."

Two nights after the landing on Tulagi, my father was nearly killed—by gunfire from the rifles of Colonel Merritt Edson's men.

"Tom and I were spending the night real close together in a foxhole," Eddie Bryan told me. Eddie Bryan had been one of my father's lieutenants; Harry Connor's letters had mentioned him.

"He had his pack on. It rained like hell that night. Edson's outfit was behind us on the high ground. And they got trigger-happy. Tom and I were really exposed. They were shooting like all get-out. Tom and I crawled out of there into a big ditch. The next day Tom wakes up and goes into his pack to get his food, and the pack is riddled with bullets. The rations were shot up."

Eddie Bryan said he was pleased to hear from me. They were good friends, he said.

"He was a real man's man—physically very, very rugged. He was an outstanding soldier. As far as commanding troops went, he knew what should be done and he knew how to tell people to do it. . . . He knew how to stick around to see how it got done."

35

Bryan's words echoed those of several other men I was able to locate subsequently.

"There were officers who would say to you, 'Hey, why don't you go over there and see where that shooting's coming from,' " George Hadzidakis told me. "Not your father. Your father would go find out for himself."

Hadzidakis, an enlisted man from New Hampshire, was with my father all the way through.

"Everything was on the level with your father," Hadzidakis told me. " 'I am your officer, therefore you'll do this' —there was never any of that crap. I've seen it with others, but with your father we never had any of that. Some officers always got a guy on the mast, you know—someone up for a court-martial or something. They got their rocks off from this. But not your father. He was no bully. He enjoyed life."

At first I wondered if the men I'd found who knew my father, thirty-five years after his death and fifty years after their war, were telling me only what they knew I wanted to hear. But with each successive man, and each successive tale, the authenticity mounted. Invariably, after I'd talked to one of them, a letter would arrive, or a snapshot—from a visit to the farm, or of the company on leave—or a list of other men to talk to.

To most of them, talking about Tom Richmond furnished a chance to go back to a time and place in their lives with which they'd long since parted company. They tossed off their various remembrances casually, entirely unaware of the effect it had on me to hear them.

A few cried upon hearing his name. Several laughed. Typical was the reaction of one man in particular, Francis Liebermann, whom I'd reached on the telephone after tracing his name through microfilmed muster roles, division directories, library telephone books, and help from his various buddies. "This is quite a shock," he said when I identified myself, and then, before I could speak again, he said, "He was the greatest company commander in the Marine Corps," lest there be any debate. I have no doubt that thousands of marines would say the same thing about their own commanders, but that knowledge did not diminish the effect such words began to have on me as they were repeated, again and again. I hadn't talked to anyone who knew my father outside of my family since I was seven. I had had no idea what to expect.

On the other hand, I'd never spoken to anyone who'd fought in the Second World War about their fighting, and in my first conversations with my father's men, something else was becoming apparent, something I hadn't anticipated: their matter-of-factness about what they'd done. Whether this reflected the great distance in time since the battles, or ambivalence about their deeds and actions in the South Pacific, their quiet and their restraint over the course of conversations with me, which often lasted several hours, furnished the first hints I'd received that heroism was not as simple as I'd always thought it to be.

Friendly fire, they told me, was a far more frequent occurrence than anyone ever admitted—especially at the beginning, when the marines had no idea what to expect and expected the worst, clouding their judgment. The emperor's troops were rumored to be a race of supermen. In the months prior, they had routed the British in Singapore, forcing the surrender of more than 60,000 British soldiers to an army half that size in a city long held to be the bastion of Western strength in the Far East. They had defeated Douglas MacArthur on the Bataan Peninsula, precipitating the humiliating and homicidal Bataan Death March of 75,000 American and Filipino prisoners.

"The Japanese were nine feet tall," Gordon Gayle said, explaining the marines' perspective. "They shot from coconut trees. From the rear. No one had ever defeated the Japanese in modern history. The first few nights were the most dangerous of the war for a lot of marines. I got shot at from a distance of ten yards or less that first night."

Francis Liebermann recalled the first moments he realized he was in a war: when the marines began to come across Japanese bodies; when a corporal and three men in his squad were killed—the 2-5's first fatalities; and when he saw the first example of the marines' having decided that it was not to be a war of gentlemanly procedure:

"I remember we captured one Jap. I don't know why the heck we didn't knock this guy off. There was a little compound down at the end of the island. The Solomons manager had a nice home up there on top of a hill. The Jap commander and his staff lived in that thing. Well, we got this one guy. Right at the edge of the water there was a little two-cell prison. It's strange. We threw him in. It had a quarter-inch steel door. Your dad said, 'Set up a guard on him.' The guy wouldn't go anywhere anyway.

"A guy named Stokes was on guard. The Jap wouldn't shut up. He kept singing, or whatever he was doing. Stokes had some armor-piercing shells in his rifle. He fired through the door. I don't know whether it killed him or not. It shut him up."

· · ·

38

The battle for the Solomons is known for more than the caves; it is known as the day the Navy deserted its marines. The Navy pulled out of the Solomons after three days, worried that the Japanese naval supremacy would wipe them out. The supply ships went with them, taking the marines' food. Over on Guadalcanal, where the Japanese had been surprised and fled the airfield without a fight to head west across the Matanikau River, captured Japanese supplies were plentiful; the daily menu featured sake and canned crab. On Tulagi, the menu offered nothing but rice.

"I still burn over Tulagi," read one of Harry Connor's letters. "If the Navy couldn't hang in there to the extent of at least landing our initial supplies, they never should have put us ashore. They plainly abandoned us. This is the reason we all went for fourteen days on one meal of captured rice."

When my father's company finally left the island to cross the bay back to Guadalcanal on a destroyer, Eddie Bryan remembers the sailors giving the marines bread and jelly—"You'd have thought it was a T-bone steak," Bryan told me.

A week after they'd landed on Guadalcanal and started their patrols up to the Japanese line on the Matanikau River, Bryan and my father stopped on a patrol one night to watch the Japanese dive-bombers attack the American ships in the bay. They watched the destroyer take a bomb down its smokestack. It broke in two, Bryan told me. No one survived.

When the 2-5 came over from Tulagi to Guadalcanal, they were designated the Division Reserve, which meant that the battalion was expected to plug every hole in the perimeter. The perimeter was huge. The marines had staked out a small section of the island, from the Matanikau River on the west to the airfield on the east—less than twenty miles across, a few miles deep. As William Manchester wrote, it was as if they had landed on Long Island and captured Jones Beach, while the Japanese had the rest of the island.

With every other unit out on the perimeter, the 2-5 was constantly on the move. "It was like the fire department," Liebermann told me. "Every time there was an attack on one part of the line, we'd get sent there. Usually it was at night. We had to move in, and if they broke through, we'd counterattack. It's a tricky thing in the jungle at night. It seemed like we were on patrol every other day, usually at night.

"The idea was to keep the Japanese from assembling any large groups. That's one of the reasons they were never able to mass any great troop strength to make the attacks —we sent combat patrols out, and if we met them, we'd take them on."

The Japanese bombing raids were frequent, if largely ineffective. There was a nightly visit from two odd-sounding Japanese planes, nicknamed Washing Machine Charlie and Louie the Louse, which would drop flares for the Japanese naval bombardments, or drop the occasional bomb themselves, to deprive the marines of their sleep.

Most of the men waited out the raids in silence. My father kept some friends with him.

"Your dad had a soy-sauce barrel he kept snakes in," Liebermann told me. "The Japanese had left these little wooden soy-sauce barrels. He knocked the end out of one of these barrels and put a cover on it. He'd keep it in his foxhole at the command post. Anybody found a snake it wound up at Tom Richmond's place.

"During these air raids he'd dump this bucket of snakes out in the hole and sit down there and play with them. He loved to do that. You can bet your ass that nobody jumped in his hole. They'd stay away from that hole."

It was not the first wartime reference I'd heard to my father and his snakes. A man named Chuck Clifford remembered my father distinctly, even though they only trained together in New River, North Carolina. The first time they met, Clifford saw my father pick up a snake and stuff it into his binocular case.

"He'd just picked the goddamned thing up," Clifford said, "and stuffed it right in there. It scared the shit out of the troops. At night a lot of people stayed away from him, with all those snakes. I used to tell people that story all the time. They'd always say, 'Oh, you're crazy. A lieutenant wouldn't do that.' But he did."

Some time later, a friend of my father's, who knew him from childhood, told me he thought my father's love of snakes represented his love of taking risks. This would certainly be in keeping with his style as a soldier, as would become eminently clear—in one case, too much so.

When the marines first landed on Guadalcanal, the Japanese were caught by surprise and fled to the west, to the other side of the Matanikau. Two weeks after the landing a headstrong marine colonel named Frank Goettge, itching for a fight, took twenty men—most of them the intelligence officers of the Fifth Marines—in a boat, circled into the bay, and landed on the other side of the spot where the Matanikau meets the ocean. There had been reports of men seeing Japanese soldiers waving a white flag. If that were true, it was a ruse. The marines were summarily slaughtered by rifle and machine-gun fire. Two survivors made it out into the bay and swam back east. They reported seeing the glint of moonlight on swords that were hacking at, and beheading, the corpses.

41

The Goettge Patrol is legendary; none of the histories would dare omit it. George MacGillivary had outlined the patrol's movements on a napkin for me in the officers' club near the Historical Center.

"The first time we crossed the Matanikau, we saw their bodies," John Babashanian, one of my father's lieutenants, told me. "All we could see was their feet sticking out of the sand and the water rolling by."

The Goettge massacre represented the second incident in the first month of fighting that let the marines know just how differently the Japanese soldier was going to fight this war. In the first, the assault at Alligator Creek, the Japanese had rushed the First Regiment's barbed-wire and machine guns with a suicidal frenzy, knowing full well they'd die in trying, and the next morning their corpses were stacked like cordwood on the sand.

Now, at the Matanikau, they were dismembering their foe.

There's a passage about a dead marine in Robert Leckie's *Helmet for My Pillow*, the memoir of a First Division veteran of Guadalcanal: "His body bore dozens of bayonet wounds. In his mouth they had stuffed flesh they had cut from his arm. His buddies said he had a tattoo there—the Marine emblem. The Japs cut it off and stuffed it in his mouth."

"We had a saying after we left the Canal and went to Australia," Babashanian told me. "As new officers joined the outfit, we used to say to them, 'You're not a man until you've crossed the Matanikau three times.' "

The Matanikau became the unofficial demarcation line

for the battle of Guadalcanal—a finger of water a couple of dozen yards across, winding its way north to the ocean, where the sandspit sticks out from the east bank, several yards wide, and diverts the river's flow.

The 2-5 was constantly engaged on the banks of the Matanikau. G Company was the vanguard company much of the time. For the first battle my father was not only in the vanguard, he was offered up for sacrifice by Colonel Merritt "Red Mike" Edson and Lieutenant Colonel Lewis "Chesty" Puller.

"Red Mike" had been promoted to command the Fifth Regiment after his Raiders had had such success on Tulagi and Edson's Ridge. Puller was the commander of the Seventh Battalion, a small, wiry, outspoken leatherneck destined to become a legend. In the bookstores today, Edson's most recent biography is called *Once a Legend*. Puller's is called *MARINE! The Life of Chesty Puller*.

Neither had time to compose a tribute to the Second Matanikau. If they had, they could have called it "The Needless Slaughter of the G-2-5." It could have been the seminal study in the capriciousness of warfare.

The arrival of Puller's Seventh Battalion gave the division command, under General Vandegrift, the confidence to start attacking instead of defending. They decided to attack the Japanese concentration on the other side of the Matanikau. It was Edson's first battle command as a regiment commander. My father was the lead pawn in his game.

The first battle started on the twenty-sixth of September. The plan was for the Raider battalion to circle inland, cross the river, and go north to take out the Japanese. The 2-5, Edson decided, would attack across the mouth of the river, across the exposed sandspit. The Seventh Battalion would circle out into the water and land on the other side, to squeeze the Japanese.

"I remember walking to that battle with your dad," Sam Bair told me. Bair was an enlisted man, my father's runner on Guadalcanal. "I was limping because I had the jungle rot on my feet. I was carrying a Springfield; he had the forty-five. He said, 'Give me your rifle and shell belt, I'll carry them, you take the forty-five.' "

I remarked that it sounded as if my father took good care of his enlisted men. Bair laughed.

"Years later, I said to him at a reunion, 'You know, the snipers were picking off the guys who had pistols. I don't know if you were doing me a favor or not.' "

Edson and Puller had no idea of the Japanese strength on the west bank of the Matanikau. On the morning of the twenty-sixth Edson ordered the G-2-5 across the sand-spit. My father led the attack, while he sent platoons across the water below him. As soon as he launched the attack, the other side of the river erupted in machine-gun, mortar, and artillery fire. The marines were defenseless. Bullets raked the water. Men died in bunches.

Harry Connor's letters include this dispatch: "26 Sept: Heavy fire from emplaced Jap machine guns and mortar. G Company attempted to gain west bank. G Co. sitting targets."

"We lost a lot of men," Don Peppard, another of my father's lieutenants, told me. "You could see them dropping. We couldn't get across. Tom was in the middle of everything."

"I was up on the high ground, placing the mortars," Eddie Bryan told me, "and your dad was out on the sand-spit. He had a hell of a time. He was pinned down, caught out on that sandspit."

That's all Eddie recalls; as he turned away to set up a mortar, a Japanese bullet hit him in the left side of his neck and exited just beneath his right ear, missing his spine by a fraction of an inch. It was the last he saw of Guadalcanal.

"My whole squad got killed behind me," Art Beres told me. "I was the only one to make it across the river. The river was alive with fire. Then I got shot. I got hit through my mouth and shoulder."

I asked him if he thought my father would have been angry at not getting across.

"Nobody made it, I know that," Beres said. "I know that for damned sure. So you didn't have to be ashamed of not making it."

Actually, Beres was wrong. One squad made it, eight men strong. One man came back.

"Yeah, we were the lead battalion, and guess who the lead company was?" Francis Liebermann said. "G-2-5. We were to go out on that exposed beach. Go down to the mouth of the Matanikau, cross on the sandbar, and get our company across and get established. We got strung out on that beach out in the open. Got one squad across. Buddy Waldron got his squad across. He was a corporal. He had, I think, seven guys. He got the whole squad across. Then the roof caved in. They shot machine guns, mortars—goddamn, they used everything. He got across. The rest of us were pinned down on that open beach. The little defilade was our only cover."

Liebermann was next to my father on the sandspit, whose beach side sloped down just enough for the men to lie flat, hug the sand, and hear the bullets passing directly over their heads.

"We laid out there on that beach for what seemed like days," Liebermann said. "It couldn't have been more than

45

a couple of hours. Our feet were almost in the water. They were machine-gunning the whole line. The bullets were hitting on our heels. If they'd been able to shoot a little higher, they would have had us all.

"And he was right there, your father. With the first platoon. We bellied our way out of that thing. Two guys got head shot. 'Stay down!' we said. 'Stay down!' They got curious. Bang—through the head."

I asked Liebermann what my father said after they'd pulled back.

"He was angry. He was angry because we lost his boys. And after we got off that spit, a fellow, a BAR [Browning automatic rifle] man, said, 'I'm going to get those sons of bitches! I'm going across to get them!' We had to physically restrain him. Four guys had to sit on him to keep him from going ape."

Not long ago my mother found a letter my father had written from Guadalcanal to his brother in November 1942. It is the only letter that exists that he wrote during the war; actually, the only letter I know of he ever wrote anyone that still exists. It is written with a fountain pen on thick paper.

"Of course, war is hell, just like they say," my father writes. "Nothing to be alarmed about, I guess, but over the period of time since we landed, I've had four officers put out of action by bullets and shrapnel, and one evacuated because of 'war hysteria.' "

Until then I hadn't fully understood a basic tenet of combat: for an officer, the statistic that matters is not the number of enemy killed but the number of men whose deaths he is responsible for. It is a unique relationship in human history, that of the man who holds the other man's life in his hands, and has to order him to die.

When my father landed on Guadalcanal, he had 151 men. When G Company left the island four months later, approximately 60 were left to walk off under their own power.

"He prayed that he'd get it, that he'd be killed, instead of so many beautiful young lieutenants," my mother told me. "These beautiful young men . . . he said it was so horrible to call and say 'I need two more lieutenants.' "

I asked Liebermann what had happened to Bud Waldron's squad.

"One was able to get into the water and swim back. He got out on the water and swam back over [in the ocean] past the mouth. He was a wreck. The rest of them . . . We didn't get them."

Why, I asked, had the G-2-5 been given the duty?

"I guess they figured if anybody could do it, Tom's outfit could. We had a pretty good reputation—that was all Tom's leadership.

"You know, the service does a lot of strange things. Bud Waldron and I had a pact. If one of us survived, the other would visit the other's parents. After I got home, I contacted Bud's folks. My mother and I went over to see them. And what they said . . . didn't happen. They had gotten Bud's body back. They got Bud's remains sent back. They'd had a funeral. But, Peter . . . no one's body got sent back from that outfit. A couple weeks later another outfit got a patrol over there, found a chain necklace he wore. Nothing else. They scoured the whole area. Nothing else."

According to the most recent of Edson's biographers, "Poor communications made things worse. Both division and Edson thought that the raiders had indicated they were across the river, so the regimental commander again launched 2/5 in the assault."

The second attack, heavily supported by Harry Connor's company, was no more successful for my father's company. After the two assaults, 25 marines had been killed or wounded.

At that point, Lyman "Buzz" Spurlock was called to Edson's post. Spurlock and my father went all the way back to New River, where they'd played all-night poker games in the abandoned farmhouse that served as the officer's club. Spurlock was the Fifth Regiment's operations officer. Edson said he wanted to personally scout the situation; Edson went down the river looking for the Raiders, and asked Spurlock to find Puller up at the mouth.

"I saw Tom, and Puller was giving him orders," Spurlock told me. "I said, 'What's the real situation there, Tom?' He told me: Buzz, I have a problem. This is the third time they want me to go across this river. I have less than fifteen effectives. The rest of the company is out there."

My father motioned toward the river, where his men lay dead and wounded.

"I told Tom to hold what he had, and as soon as I talked to Edson I'd get around to him," Spurlock told me. "Edson went inland. Tom held fast. He was holding the spit."

• • •

Later, I found an account of the battle in a book I pulled randomly off a shelf at the Marine Corps Historical Center. I copied the page, but neglected to copy the title page, and have since been unable to locate it again. The passage is a description of the battle at the mouth of the Matanikau.

It was about 1400 Saturday September 26 and the lead scout was about to step from the sandspit into the stream bordering the village when a barrage of grenades flung by mortars burst on all sides. . . . Light machine guns were quickly broken out and everyone who could bring his weapon to bear opened fire. Several hundred yards downstream, the rear of the column was hit by a rain of grenades, then fired on by hidden riflemen and gunners across the stream.

Everyone went to the ground while Puller ordered Walker Reaves to deploy alongside the river and mount a direct assault across the sandspit. Reaves ordered Capt. Tom Richmond's Company to attack through E Company. The lead G Company platoon, under 2nd Lt. Paul Moore, dropped into the water several hundred yards south of the sandspit. One of Moore's Marines was hit just as he reached the lee of the west bank. As the rest of the platoon withdrew, Moore swam to the west bank to rescue the wounded man.

What probably kept Paul Moore alive, he told me, was not being moved until the next day, when the corpsmen found him. The doctors told him if his heart had been expanding instead of contracting when the bullet went through his chest, he'd have died. He was sent home to give speeches at munitions factories and encourage people to make bombs.

When I located Paul Moore, he was the Right Reverend Paul Moore, the recently retired bishop of the Episcopal Diocese of New York. Moore won a Silver Star for his actions on Guadalcanal, and later gained fame as an antiwar spokesman during the Vietnam era. His home in Manhattan features a framed cover of *Newsweek* that shows him addressing an antiwar rally in Washington.

When I asked Moore why he'd enlisted, he said, "I consulted my parish priest. He'd been in the First World War. And he told me that it was better to go than not to."

Considering his eventual fame as an antiwar cleric, I asked Paul Moore if he had any ambivalence about his old feelings for the marines. "There was enough positive emotional stuff—being a hero, being in the right war—to counteract the other stuff," he told me.

But when I first talked to Moore on the telephone, and asked him about the first assault on the Matanikau, his language wasn't particularly holy.

"We were under the terrible leadership of Chesty Puller," he said. "He was an asshole. A real shit."

I asked Spurlock about the wisdom of ordering the G-2-5 across the open spit.

"You couldn't have gotten a thousand men across that river," Spurlock told me.

The battle that Hersey documented in *Into the Valley* took place in and down the Matanikau, where the river narrows and gets lost in a valley wrapped in thick jungle. According to my father's soldiers, Hersey had it wrong; G and E companies led the attack into the valley, and H Company, the machine-gun support company, blundered its way into a bad situation where the creek meets the river.

It was here in October, Connor's letters said, that G Company took heavy casualties coming up through the middle of E while John Hersey chronicled the exploits of H Company under Rigaud.

"Rigaud—that's a bunch of bullshit, if you want to put it plainly," Liebermann told me. "You know who was up there? Tom Richmond's company. Can you imagine H Company out in front of the attack? H Company was a machine-gun company. Charlie Rigaud was a hotdog anyway. We were up there doing the fighting and he was sitting there with his machine guns.

"That's the reason your father never got any of the credit he was due for what he got done—he was a quiet, behind-the-scenes sort of guy. And that was the thing that always burned my butt: he never was recognized for the accomplishments he made. I've told anybody who listened about them, too. Ever since."

The afternoon before the 2-5 crossed the river in the valley, Liebermann was surprised to get a tap on his shoulder from a runner from battalion headquarters. He had no idea what it was about. They were set to jump off across the river in the morning.

Major Lew Walt, the battalion commander, gathered Liebermann and two other men in his tent.

"You fellas have all been recommended for promotion to second lieutenant," Walt told them. My father hadn't even told Liebermann he was going to get him promoted. Liebermann and the other two accepted the promotions.

"Then I hope you live through your first day as a second

lieutenant," Walt told them, and sent them back into the valley.

My own arrival is less dramatic. It takes forty-two hours after leaving New York, by way of Fiji and Vanuatu, over inconceivably vast planes of empty ocean. The last hop is on Solomon Airways' 737, with the name GUADALCANAL painted on the nose; the nation is several months behind on its payments, and is about to lose the plane.

I land at the airfield where the Pacific war began, Henderson Field. A cadre of immigration officers of the republic of the Solomon Islands, noting that I have identified myself as a journalist, confiscate my passport and my return ticket and instruct me to report to immigration headquarters in downtown Honiara, the city that has grown up around the spot where the Matanikau flows north into the ocean.

I ask them why I can't settle things at the airport. They tell me I am welcome to get back on the plane and leave immediately. I agree to go downtown.

They are an exotic, wildly beautiful people, the Melanesians. Their features belong to the ancestral pulls of a different earth than mine. In a cinder-block office in the government compound downtown, these Melanesians do not appear to be happy. A grim man smoking a cigarette, surrounded by several grim assistants, asks me in pidgin English what it is I am doing on Guadalcanal. I show him a photograph of my father on the island, and his letter, his war records. The man's staff begins to crowd around us, looking through the file. Bristly expressions loosen into huge smiles.

52

"First Marine Division?" says one. I nod. They smile and nod back.

"I don't think there will be a problem," says the man with the cigarette.

Just down the road from the government offices sits the Solomon Kitano Mendana, one of three hotels in the capital city. I retire to the patio, with its view across a small bay of the spit of land where the Port of Honiara is located —Point Cruz. With something of a start, I realize that I am sitting, drinking a beer, on the piece of land across which my father led his company to attack Point Cruz in the fourth battle of the Matanikau River.

Chickens are grazing in the hotel courtyard; the electricity is sporadic. There is no television in the Solomons, but the Mendana has an in-house video service. The first night it features an American low-budget horror movie featuring a scene where a young woman turns on her shower and blood comes out of the showerhead.

The Mendana's amenities include two bars and a private function room called the Coastwatchers' Lounge, named for the Australians who watched the horizon for attacking Japanese ships and planes.

"[Dedicated] to the memory of the brave band of men who operated behind the lines as intelligence gatherers during the Second World War," reads the hotel's promotional literature—a nice sentiment, but unusual, considering that the Mendana Hotel is owned and operated by the Kitano Construction Company, founded by Tjsuguto Kitano in 1946 and now one of Japan's largest building concerns.

• • •

53

The lobby of the American embassy is stacked with boxes of files, a lawn mower, and a spare tire. The Americans are leaving. The embassy is closing.

"Your father was here when the flag went up, and you're here as the flag comes down," Allen Bishop observes in his empty office. The acting chargé d'affaires, himself a veteran of eight and a half years in the Corps, Bishop explains in subdued fashion that the embassy is closing at the end of the week, the victim of budget cuts mandated by the Bush administration: the president who had campaigned on his war record in the Pacific authorized the closing of the embassy on the island where the marines had won the Pacific war for the United States.

This is not entirely surprising. The war in the Pacific theater never captured the American public's imagination, and the closing of the Solomon embassy, Bush knew, would cause nary a ripple. The European war is what riveted most Americans, whose ancestral homelands were being devoured in 1942; in the South Pacific, Asian armies were conquering Pacific islands, marching through a geography that held no significance to the average American. On paper, the Japanese intent was to capture the oil fields of the Netherlands East Antilles to power their war efforts; in fact, the Japanese fully intended to capture Australia, cut off Allied shipping lanes to the Mideast, and then invade Hawaii, holding 400,000 American citizens hostage, to force a quick American surrender.

Within the military, of course, the name of Guadalcanal has survived. In the corps it is legend.

"Every young marine cuts his teeth on stories of Guadalcanal," Bishop says. "I hope we can reestablish the embassy. They're a very pro-American people."

In its fifteenth year of independence from the United

Kingdom, the republic of the Solomon Islands is, by some accounts, the poorest nation in the entire South Pacific Forum—Vanuatu, Tonga, the Republic of Kiribati, all of them trying to attract outside investment and repel the rape of their remaining finite resources by their larger neighbors, who crave the timber of their forests.

As Bishop and I talk, the electricity suddenly goes off all over the city. A phone rings in another office. Bishop hurries to answer it. Three days before the closing, he is hoping it's a reprieve from Washington.

It isn't. It is a fax he's requested: a map of the island, pointing out various war memorials and sites to visit. He hands it to me and invites me to attend the final lowering of the flag, on Friday.

I want to visit Tulagi. Down at the airport, by the side of the runway, I find an air charter company owned by an Australian army pilot named Dick Grouse, who came to Guadalcanal years ago, bought a fifty-year-old Grumman seaplane and a Bell helicopter, and makes a living hiring out to foresters and divers from Australia, New Zealand, and Malaysia. He'd be glad to fly me over to Tulagi.

After a twenty-minute flight we set down in the middle of the old British cricket field, from the days of the British Solomon Islands—before the Japanese took them without a fight. Village children gather at the field's edge to watch our descent. On the north side of the field, at the base of a hill, the Raiders buried 47 of their dead. The Raiders always buried their own.

A half-mile away, at Beach Blue, where the marines landed on Tulagi, a single American landing barge rests at peace, rusting, nosed onto the white sand, surrounded by seashells; in the shallows of the cove a man fishes with a bow and arrow. A few yards inland the terrain rises steeply; the hillside is pocked by dark caves.

It is a lovely cove. As I walk across the deck of the barge, I hear a chorus of schoolchildren singing in the wooden schoolhouse with open windows just a few yards from the beach.

The caves are like many eyes—dark, unblinking. Some of the caves could fit two or three men; some could fit a dozen. Vines and grasses conceal some of the openings; others yawn, bottomless.

We take off from the cricket field and circle over an adjacent island, where the shell of a Japanese destroyer sits sunken in a couple of fathoms of water. The water is brilliant aquamarine; the hulk of the destroyer is a stunningly bright red-gold rust; the colors in the hulk, an elongated gravestone, a two-hundred-foot coffin, are the colors of autumn leaves back where I come from. The deck sits two or three feet below the water, as if preserved in turquoise aspic.

Back at Henderson Field, I thank Grouse for the ride. As we walk out of his hangar, I motion to a pile of debris on the other side of a chain-link fence, and to three cargo containers, the kind of containers you see cranes taking off of freighters on the docks of Newark. Elsewhere in the overgrown half-acre lot are strewn a few piles of lumber, a few broken trucks, and pieces of fighter planes.

Presiding over this curious tableau is a potbellied man with a ruddy, distinctly Western face.

"That's Patrick Murphy," says Dick Grouse. "He's an American."

"I should meet him," I say. Dick Grouse doesn't say anything. His silence is conspicuous.

My Father's War

• • •

One of my brothers, Tom, my father's first son, thinks my father kept the bloody Japanese flag to remind him of his worst failure in the war, based on a story I'd never heard before. My brother says my mother once told him to never ask our father about the war, because one time he was on a patrol somewhere and nearly all of his men were killed when he led them into an ambush. Afterward, went the tale, my father and the remaining two or three men managed to fool the Japanese patrol into thinking they were surrounded, and they captured them.

"He felt responsible," my brother told me. "And I think he kept the stuff, not as a token of success, but to remember that ambush for the rest of his life. To remember that his blood was the same as Japanese blood."

The ambush could have easily happened. One of my father's men told me how heedless they'd been at the beginning, using the same trails day after day on patrol until, as he put it, "eventually it cost us."

It cost the crew of the Jezebel. It's a Sherman tank, sitting at the bottom of a valley of eight-foot-high grass surrounded by steep hills on three sides, a mile off the road. A huge hole is torn from the armor in its back; a shell had knocked the tread off the wheels, and it was done. The tank had no business being here; the valley was miles behind Japanese lines, and no battles were fought in this hollow. But that was the nature of this war; patrols split off, got lost. It was often a matter of men meeting men in the middle of nowhere. It was hard to find your way home. It was hard for the marines to honor their code of retrieving bodies.

A soldier in my father's company named Bill Lynch won

the Navy Cross for an act of heroism that cost him his life. My father couldn't find his body in the jungle. The following year, after the island had been captured and the army was using it as a base, my father returned to the island and tried to find Lynch's body. You had to retrieve the body if you could if you were a marine. Marines always recovered the bodies. He didn't find it.

JEZEBEL is written on the tank's turret. Both front hatches are open, frozen where they'd been flung open, either by the crew trying to escape or the Japanese trying to get in, and the armor around them is scarred by bullets.

The turret's top hatch is gone; the inside of the turret bears the marks of a thousand bullets. It was a massacre.

The only sound in the valley is the call of the mynah bird. Its cry spans an octave. It does not sound like a bird at all; it sounds like a man imitating a bird. I find my eyes combing the hillsides. I see nothing but sun and grass. I walk out of the valley fairly quickly.

Farther down the east-west road, I turn down a side road randomly and find, just as the road is turning into a path, a strange structure by the side of the road. A monument of sorts. The plaque on the structure says that it's a monument marking the spot where the Japanese began their march east to retake Henderson Field. As I read the inscription, the sweat is rolling off my nose and blotting the ink in my notebook. If they started the walk here, an hour's drive from the airport, I can't begin to imagine what the march through the grass must have been like. I have a fleeting thought of walking into the high grass, just for a minute; I can't move more than five feet before the foliage stops me. I would need more than a machete to make progress; I would need a chainsaw.

As I get back into my car, a large bird leaps out of the

crest of a palm, loudly, and coasts to another group of palms. It's a bald eagle.

On my drive back to town I pass a truck with the words EXPLOSIVE ORDNANCE DISPOSAL UNIT written on its side.

The final assault across the Matanikau took out Point Cruz in the first week of November. The 2-5 crossed the river south and inland, circled around my hotel, and assaulted the point. They backed the Japanese up to the point, and off it. They killed 239 Japanese, including a full colonel and 18 other officers, and captured 9 field guns and 34 machine guns.

"Ended up in close range grenade and pistol battle," Harry Connor's diary reads. "No prisoners."

After my father fought on Guadalcanal, his evaluation was written by Lieutenant Colonel Lew Walt. At that point, Walt had not achieved the legendary status that would be awarded him later in the war and long afterward; when Walt retired in 1971, he was assistant commandant of the Marine Corps, a four-star general, and the top-ranking marine in Vietnam.

Such evaluations by superior officers were a routine part of military life. In the "Report on Fitness of Officers of the United States Marine Corps," there are four sections. The first is "fitness," with eleven subcategories: physical fitness; military bearing and neatness; attention to duty; cooperation; initiative; intelligence; judgment and common sense; presence of mind; force; leadership; and loyalty. The possible rankings for each trait are "unsatisfactory," "fair," "good," "very good," "excellent," and "outstanding."

The second section determines the degree of his commanding officer's desire to have him in his outfit: "Considering the possible requirements of the service in war," it asks, "indicate your attitude toward having this officer under your command. Would you (a) particularly desire to have him? (b) be glad to have him? (c) be willing to have him? (d) prefer not to have him?"

The third section is a blank three lines, to be used for a candid evaluation of the officer.

The fourth section is one blank line, to be used for a general evaluation of the man.

After Guadalcanal, Lew Walt gave my father nine "excellents" and two "outstandings"—in "physical fitness" and "loyalty." (I would learn later that the loyalty grade was the most important in evaluating a marine officer's fitness for advancement.) He would "particularly desire to have him." In his remarks Walt wrote, "See confidential letter under separate cover."

The confidential letter read, "This officer is outstanding as a leader in combat against the enemy. He is fearless, energetic, and cool under fire. As a company commander on Tulagi and Guadalcanal he displayed the highest degree of combat efficiency."

The hills are too full of shadows here in the valley. It could have come from anywhere, the enemy fire. In the middle of the river a woman does her laundry; children play on the rocks; on every side the jungle slopes upward. I have been told that there are Japanese caves on the other side of the river, up in the hills. I don't look for them. The jungle is dark and impenetrable on the brightest of days here. I can hear voices, but I can see no one in the foliage.

"On Guadalcanal one time I heard his voice somewhere down the line, in the jungle," George Hadzidakis told me. "You couldn't see him, but you know how sometimes you can hear someone's voice? Suddenly I heard your father say, 'I'm telling you, after this war is over, I'm going to come back with a jeep and a barrel of beer. Then I'm gonna drink it and piss all over this island.' "

A half-mile away, there's a dusty village called Chinatown on the banks of the river, and on its main street sits the Mataniko Saloon and Bar. It's the darkest bar I've ever been in. Its windows are barred. Its floors are concrete. Its walls are riveted steel plates, stained with what appear to be expectorations of betel nut. On each side of the room sits a cement picnic table. In the middle of the room, enclosed in his own room behind more bars, sits a man. He sits next to a large cooler.

When I walk in in the middle of the afternoon, I stand and wait for my eyes to adjust to the gloom, and around me the beery conversation wanes to silence. The man in the cage stares at me a long time. A very long time. Then he sells me a can of Victoria beer.

At one of the tables sit three men under whose table stands a pyramid of perhaps a hundred empty beer cans, very possibly more. The other table holds three older men, all quite drunk. They ask me to join them. I do. One of them asks what I am doing there. I tell him that my father had fought here.

"First Marine Division?" one asks. I nod. I tell them he fought *right* here—out back, a dozen yards behind the bar, in that water—in the shallows of the river, littered with trash; it's an ignoble site, the shallow, weed-choked channel that sits behind the backs of the Chinatown stores. I have waded down there already and stirred up the mosquitoes; the malarial mosquitoes come out at dusk. Their bodies are green, and they feel sinister when they light on your skin.

"This place is far from being crocodile-infested, as some press releases might make you believe," my father wrote in his letter to his brother. "But some parts of it often remind me of Kipling's 'Great green greasy Limpopo River, all set about with fever trees.' "

My father never lost his malaria. It would revisit him the rest of his life, send him into a darkened room where, beneath layers of blankets, he'd shiver with the fever.

The men in the Mataniko do not know that they are getting drunk a few yards from the site of some of the worst firefights of the battle. I try to make them understand, but they just smile, showing their black teeth, and hoist their cans of Victoria beer. They had never tasted beer, the men of the Solomons, until the British arrived in the thirties.

I cannot raise a toast to Harry Connor here. As I walk out of the door, one of the men at my table turns to the other table and says, "First Marine Division," but I don't think the men at the other table paid any notice.

Chinatown is on the old east-west road, the trail the marines used most frequently to get to the Matanikau. Now it holds two Chinese restaurants and a casino where, I'm told, the tourists go to find women. One night I dine in one of the Chinese restaurants. "Auld Lang Syne" filters through the speakers. It is August.

"Have a little jungle music every once in a while," my father's letter said. "One of my men picked up a guitar from a Navy plane which went a-reef over in Tulagi. When we go out on a mission we leave the guitar with company property in the rear echelon. Then when we settle down in a new line position or bivouac area, out comes the guitar and a songfest gets under way. The man who plays it is really talented. Good for the morale."

The man was named Al Carbuto. He went on to publish a march called "Get Your Gear On (We're Moving Out)." According to a magazine clip from 1944 about the "Foxhole Tunesmith"—sent to me by Theron Cordray, another man in the G-2-5—the song became something of an anthem in the First Marine Division, with verses along the lines of "Now when we're home and settled down we'll hear no more of gear / All we want to hear is 'Come and get your beer!' " Cordray also sent me a page of lyrics from another Carbuto song, untitled: "We fight and sweat the whole day through / for the good ole U.S.A. / We are proud of our great title / The United States Marines / And when our mission has been done / There will be no rising sun / Here's a toast to Old Glory / As we fight for our corps."

Morale was an issue, of course. But Leonard Lawton told me, "Morale was always high. Yessir. Even on October 14, Navy Day, we got a message we heard on the radio service of the Navy that Forrestal was talking through all the static. We heard, 'We hope, we think we can keep Guadalcanal.' That didn't bother us. We thought, 'He doesn't know we're in charge here.' We heard that and it didn't shake us at all. We continued to have high morale no matter what."

One morning on a sidewalk outside of the national bank in Honiara, I am greeted by a hallucination: an elderly man—a white man wearing white shorts, white kneesocks, a white shirt, and a hat out of whose band curls a long emu feather. The only color in his ensemble is furnished by his green-and-orange-striped regimental belt and the scarlet capillaries lacing his regimental visage.

"You have to keep the flag flying!" he tells me in regimental British tones. "You're not pulling out of the Solomon Islands—you're pulling out of Guadalcanal!"

I have happened upon the island's most tangible living link to the world I'm pursuing. Bill Guinan tells me he is the director of prisons for the government of the Solomon Islands. He was the governor of Wandsworth Prison in London when the queen dispatched him to the Solomons a decade ago to quell a series of prison riots.

But Bill Guinan is no warden; that's just a job. He is a soldier. He fought the Japanese in India for the Fifty-fourth Regiment—"The Flamers, you know; we burned New York when the Dutch wouldn't give it up"—and finished in 1945, guarding MacArthur in Tokyo. Guinan remembers pitched battles in India. He remembers killing Japanese. He remembers how many he killed. But his respect for his enemy, he tells me, never diminished.

"Someone asked MacArthur if he had a choice to assemble an army out of any soldiers on earth," Guinan tells me, "and he said, 'All my private soldiers would be Japanese' " —because they played by different rules. They lured marines into ambushes by waving white flags. Their snipers harnessed themselves into the tops of palm trees to keep their bodies from plummeting to earth after they'd been killed, so that the marines would keep shooting and expend ammunition. They would feign death on the battlefield and then, with a surprise grenade, take a marine's life, and their own; the marines took to stabbing every corpse over again, just in case.

Once, my mother said, my father told her he'd been cut off from his patrol in the jungle and had met a lone Japanese soldier. He looked the man in the eye, hoping the other man would see his plea: *We can just both keep walking.* But the Japanese soldier, steeled in a different combat ethic, pulled his knife, and my father had to pull his, and killed him. I always figured that explained the blood on the flag. But I don't really know; there may be another explanation, as I learned much later. I got a call from Bill Looney. He said he wanted to read me a letter he'd gotten from another one of my father's men on Guadalcanal. Looney had mentioned my project to Randall Borough, another of my father's men, in a passing conversation, and Borough had written back and told Looney about my father's solo night patrols.

When he was on Guadalcanal, Borough told Looney, my father would go out at night, on his own, on solo patrols to kill Japanese. He told Borough that none of his superiors ever knew about it, nor any of the men beneath him. He only told Borough several months later, over drinks in Australia. Borough said that the next day, when he asked my father about it, my father refused to speak of it.

"This is the bravest guy I ever met in the war," Borough told Looney.

Perhaps, I thought, it hadn't been true. Perhaps it had been a boast. No one else ever mentioned anything about his one-man guerilla patrols, and I'd talked to nearly 100 of them. On the other hand, nothing any of them told me suggested he was a man given to boasting—as a rule, he was just the opposite.

No, it was just as likely, I think, that he did exactly what he'd told Borough he'd done—perhaps to seek revenge for the men he'd lost, perhaps because the Japanese disregard for life had empowered him to become cold, ruthless, and efficient. Maybe if you were going to fight in a war, and you had it within you to do so, you had to do absolutely everything you could, and get yourself to the place where there are no rules. Perhaps on Guadalcanal, one-man patrols to kill Japanese was the height of bravery, and to ask your men to go along with you would have been unfair.

I do not ever allow myself to think that, if what he told Borough was accurate, he enjoyed it, because I'm sure he didn't. My mother once told me that when he first came home from the war my father said, "We're not going to have children. I won't bring children into a world where people kill each other." Fortunately for me, he changed his mind. It did not occur to me that he might have been talking about himself—that perhaps he had decided that whatever kind of man he was after fighting in the South Pacific, he did not want to pass it on.

But the look of pleading on Bill Guinan's face and the desperate conviction in his voice—and the words and stories of all of the others I talked to—have assured me that whatever it was my father did on Guadalcanal, it was necessary, and anything else that it may have been is irrelevant.

As Guinan talks, a Benson & Hedges burns down between the second and third fingers of his left hand. The tip of his emu feather is dangerously close to the glowing ash; he does not notice.

"Guadalcanal must never be forgotten," he says. But he is no longer talking to me; he is talking aloud, to himself.

"They've bloody well forgotten it. But it must never be forgotten."

"I've got the bones of this one in the container," Patrick Murphy tells me. "Want to see them?"

I have at last met the man supervising those cargo containers at the airstrip. We are standing next to a pile of twisted aluminum fragments of various shapes that used to be a Japanese Zero. Now it looks like a mound of metal shavings.

"Sure," I say. I assume that the "bones" are the metal skeletal infrastructure of the Zero. I am wrong. Patrick Murphy ducks into one of the cargo containers and comes out with a brown cardboard box that bears a white label. The top of the label is covered by Japanese characters beneath which, in black block letters, is the English translation:

JAPANESE REMAINS PERSON. BRAVE MAN ZERO FIGHTER.

Murphy begins to remove the tape from the box. He has the tan and the physique of the weekend golfer who spends more time with the postgame beers than he does exercising. Finding him here with his detritus is like running into the loquacious stranger you did your best not to engage in conversation last month at the video store in a suburban Virginia mall.

"You don't have to open it," I say.

He shrugs, puts the box on a chair in the sun, and comes back to my side. Patrick Murphy's business card reads, "Solomon Islands WWII Museum," but to this point the museum consists of the three metal cargo containers that arrived from Erlanger, Kentucky, in 1992, and several pieces of destroyed airplanes strewn about a half-acre lot: propellers, wingtips, fuel tanks, odd struts—and an old car under the hood of which toils one of Patrick Murphy's native assistants.

"This looks like a pile of shit to you," he says, nodding at the Zero wreckage. "I can make this airplane fly."

There is only one fighter plane in very good condition on the island of Guadalcanal. It is an American Wildcat. It resides at the Vilu Village War Museum—a collection of various pieces of wreckage that sits in a field forty kilometers down the road. Patrick Murphy has offered the native proprietor of the museum, Selwyn Ramoibeu, good money for the plane. Ramoibeu will not sell it.

Still, it is Patrick Murphy's intent, he says, to turn the island into the world's biggest museum. He intends to salvage and restore 25 of the 450 airplanes he claims to have located in the Solomon Islands. He will sell some of them. He will keep the others, and hire them out to pilots who want to come to the Solomons and engage in mock dogfights. He will recreate the battle, and charge people a lot of money to mock-fight it all over again.

"I have forty-five letters of intent already," he tells me. "They've been doing it for two years in California, and they get fourteen hundred dollars a flight."

Patrick Murphy doesn't blame the Solomon government for its reluctance to allow people to export memorabilia: "Hey, sixty years ago they were eating each other. Give them credit. They've spent the last fifty years with people coming in and ripping people off. Guadalcanal has been the rich boys' parts store. Most of the expats are bullshit artists. They don't want to teach. They just leave. Like the loggers.

"But I'm not here to do this and run away. I want to

teach people, and here the people actually want to learn something. Not like the States. Nobody wants to learn in America anymore."

When I ask Patrick Murphy why he left the States, he says, "It got real complicated back home."

He poses for a photograph with a piece of the Zero wing.

"Put the bones back in, will you?" he calls to his assistant. "Otherwise they'll start to stink." He turns to me. "And they will stink," he says with a shake of his head, as if it were the pilot's fault, and not his.

I find Selwyn Ramoibeu at the gate to the Vilu Village War Museum. It is a swinging gate, crossing a rutted dirt road, a couple of hundred yards off the main road, where I found a hand-painted sign for the museum nailed to a tree. The sign that greets me at the gate asks for a donation of five Solomon dollars. Selwyn approaches the gate and apologizes: He needs to ask for money because the government will give him no funds; of course, the government has no money at all anyway.

And still, he tells me, when Patrick Murphy offered to buy the Wildcat, there was no question about it: he'd never sell.

"It belongs here," he says. "We brought it here from the jungle." Selwyn has a face that betrays no age; he could be twenty-five, he could be fifty. All of the angles of his face suggest that a smile is its natural expression.

His collection at the museum has been hauled out of the clotted jungle, gathered with the help of friends and relatives, and it includes Japanese and American wrecks alike; a Japanese tank, parts of American planes, cannons and bullets and helmets. The Wildcat. Selwyn is proud of his wreckage. With delight, he shows me how the wings of the Wildcat still fold in, like the wings of a bird nestling against its breast, for storage below decks on a carrier.

Selwyn clearly enjoys curating the collection. There is a reason for this: his father fought with the marines at the Matanikau River. So did mine, I say. Our fathers may have fought together. He offers to introduce me to his father.

Up the road, Barnabas Ramoibeu walks out of his grass hut holding a Bible. A marine sergeant's stripes were tattooed onto his left shoulder fifty years ago. "The marines tattooed," Barnabas Ramoibeu tells me.

He is carrying a book about the battle, written in pidgin, published in the Solomons. It is a history of the Guadalcanal natives who helped the marines. Its title is the name of the battle, as the natives have always referred to it: *The Big Death*.

"I shoot Japanese," he says, smiling; his teeth are the color of a midnight sky. "My country asks me to fight. I say, 'I can do that.' "

Around his neck, on a rainbow-colored ribbon, he wears a medal. It's not a heavy medal, not molded out of serious stuff. I heft it, and it's as light as plastic. It is plastic. At a ceremony on the occasion of the fiftieth anniversary of the battle, representatives of the United States gave them to all the surviving Melanesians who fought in the battle.

Selwyn tells me that there's some wreckage that isn't on the map. He tells me there's a wrecked bomber on top of a mountain. His friend Peter found the plane last year. I tell him I'd like to see it. He casts a skeptical eye my way. It is a long walk, he says. I can take it, I tell him. He tells me to wear boots.

"We have many snakes," Selwyn had told me.
My father must have been in heaven.

A few days later Selwyn Ramoibeu leaves a painstakingly
written note at my hotel: if I meet them at dawn, his friend
Peter Alu will take us up the mountain at the western end
of the island to see the wreckage of the American airplane.
I don't like crashed planes. But I have never seen a B-17
and I have never climbed a jungle mountain.

The sun is just over the horizon when, at the foot of the
mountain, Peter pulls a knife and two machetes from his
bag and hands one machete to Selwyn. Peter leads, Selwyn
follows me.

Peter is a hunter of pigs by trade. As a sidelight, like
many natives, Peter collects artifacts of the battles. He
owns some of the marines' eating utensils, Selwyn tells me.
Peter doesn't tell me; he doesn't talk much—a little pidgin,
and his own dialect. Peter found the plane during the
weeklong anniversary celebration attended by several
dozen veterans last year. He saw a helicopter circling the
top of the mountain peak for two days. He'd heard the
stories of a bomber crashing on a mountaintop. It took
him two days to find it.

We start up, through a field. Spiderwebs snag my face;
spiders sit huddled in the webs, their bodies huge and vi-
brant with reds and yellows. I am forever clawing at the
filaments.

"The spiders helped the marines to beat the Japanese,"
Selwyn tells me. "If the American patrols were looking for
the Japanese, walking through the jungle, and there were
no spiders, they would know that the Japanese had been

71

there. But if there were webs, then no one had been
through that trail."

I am wearing heavy boots; my guides are barefoot, and
climb the slope with easy agility as it winds upward. Selwyn, I know, has no climbing shoes because he can afford
none. At any rate, barefoot, I think, is the best way to
negotiate the jungle foliage, which grows out of the soil at
impossible angles. We have climbed to an altitude of at
least two thousand feet, but the jungle floor is thick with
grass and plants and vines and trees.

At one point, Peter stops and turns and bends down to
hoist me up to a ledge, and I see the dog tags hanging from
his neck. I ask him about them. He found them near the
wreckage. I record the name of the flyer in my notebook.

The jungle is thick and dark; the canopy of trees blots
the sun. The vines grab at my feet. At times I can't see ten
feet in either direction for the vines and the trees and the
brush. The jungle is fragrant with the duel between decay
and life. My clothes are soaked through, and I feel muscles
I never knew I had.

It takes three hours to reach the crest and another thirty
minutes to slide down into the crater on our backs, grab-
bing roots and vines, before a glint of aluminum flashes
through the shadows, and then another, and suddenly the
wreckage is everywhere. A section of the fuselage has come
to rest pointing straight up, held up by trees, the most
unnatural position an airplane could ever assume. Farther
down the hill lies the bomber's nose, a word stenciled on
it: ESTHER. In the mulch of the jungle floor I find a piece of
the wing. It has a six-digit number on it. I record it. I find
a piece of the tail; small bullet holes dot it in clusters. I find
the place in the fuselage where the roof gunner stood in his
glass bubble.

Preserved beneath the jungle's canopy, the pieces of the plane are in remarkable condition; it feels as if the plane could have crashed last week. Aluminum doesn't rust. It is astonishingly thin and malleable, the aluminum that made up the skin of the wings and the fuselage—slight and improbably frail. It seems remarkable that this could have been a B-17. But farther down the hill I come across a piece of rusted iron, a small piece, and it's as heavy as the core of the earth. It's a piece of a radial engine.

Selwyn finds the cockpit radio. The dial is turned to INTER. He asks me what it means. I tell him that the B-17 was a very big plane, with a crew of nine, and that on this mission, as the aircraft fell, the pilot's last words were on his intercom, to his crew.

Peter tells me, in one of his few voluntary offerings, that I am the second white man to see this. The first, he says, came to take away two skeletons. This means that there may be another seven of them left to be found.

Then I find an unexploded bullet shell jammed into a knot of a tree, about a foot off the ground. It could not have landed there by chance. Peter takes it and puts it in his bag. Selwyn wonders how it got in the tree. Perhaps, I say, a crewman crawled away from the wreck, knowing that the Japanese would find it first, but wanted to leave a clue as to what direction he'd gone just in case an American patrol came through.

Ten yards farther away in the same direction, Peter starts digging through the mulch on the jungle floor.

"What is this?" he asks. He hands me a square piece of iron.

"It's a belt buckle," I say. "Don't dig there anymore."

• • •

73

The descent is quicker but still arduous, and when we return to the bottom of the mountain, I open the trunk of my car and pull out three beers. I hand one to each of my guides. I slump to the ground and lean my back against one wheel of the rental car.

I raise a toast to Harry Connor.

That evening, as I sift through my notes on the patio of the hotel, I consider that, with the serial number, the name on the nose, and the name on Peter's dog tags, I can trace the B-17's history when I get back to the States. But it occurs to me that if I do so, the family of the man whose dog tags are now bouncing around Peter Alu's neck might want them back, and I realize that where they are now is where they should be. There could be no stronger memorial to the dead flyer's efforts.

I will lose the serial number of the B-17.

Five days after my arrival, the flag comes down.

The ceremony is brief. Allen Bishop invites the attendees to finish the beer in the embassy refrigerator. One beer loosens Bishop's demeanor, but he's still not smiling. He says that Bill Guinan paid a surprise visit that afternoon, carrying a Japanese helmet he'd just bought off a collector. "To humiliate me," Bishop says. Bishop did not appreciate the subtext of Guinan's gesture: that half a century later the Americans were surrendering the island back to the Japanese. "He said to me, 'The people here don't see you as closing the embassy. They see you as running away.' "

Allen Bishop paused for a sip of Victoria.

"And in a way," he said, "I can see their point."

Shortly after my father's death, my mother asked the police to come and take away his rifles, and they did. The medals went into a safe-deposit box. No one knows what happened to the machine gun. The uniform in the trunk became the birthplace for a litter of kittens and was ruined and discarded. The Japanese flag disappeared.

Photographs, letters, papers—if they existed, they were lost. We did keep the portrait of my father in uniform, painted just after the war by a man named Alphaeus Cole, who died in the Chelsea Hotel several years ago at the age of 112. In the portrait my father has ribbons on his chest. He is a handsome and serious man. That portrait hangs in my home now. It makes it easier for me to be a father to my son. It allows me to instill in him something that I cannot give him: the moral certitude of heroism in the face of adversity.

But for the most part, we were not a good family for keeping track of things after he died. Possessions scattered. No one felt the overwhelming need to be reminded of his absence once he was gone.

One of my father's brothers died shortly before my father's death, of cancer, and my father's other brother died soon after it, also of cancer. His widowed mother, having outlived all four of her sons—one died in infancy, of polio —died soon after that. My mother sold the farm to the Girl Scouts and married again and moved the family into Manhattan; a fatherless family in Bronxville, a tiny place constructed entirely of symmetrical two-parent families like interlocking building blocks, was an oddity. We veered off onto a completely different track, a family without a foundation to anchor it.

Several decades later, after I'd married and had two children, the four of us moved into a house in upstate New York, out in the country, in a valley with just a few farmhouses. The first time we looked at the house, I went down to the basement, where, on an empty table that had once been the home to a model-train layout, there was a cardboard box that, according to its label, had once contained a scoutmaster's uniform. We bought the house and we live there now.

I hung the portrait of my father in our living room, so that my son and daughter, who never met their grandfather, would know him as a marine. I don't know if that's what he would have wanted, but in a short forty-four years on earth, I reasoned, a man does not leave too many marks, and I was certain that his had not been made as the president of the Custom-Made Paper Bag Company. The family crest he designed didn't feature a paper bag; it featured a coiled rattlesnake, two autumn leaves, the Marine Corps symbol, the words "Semper Fidelis" and the shoulder patch of the First Marine Division.

The patch was issued to the men after the Guadalcanal campaign. It was the first combat patch of the Pacific war. It shows a red numeral 1 on a field of blue, surrounded by five white stars that signified the Southern Cross, at which the marines would gaze as they waited in their foxholes for the bombs or the bayonet.

I have saved the ridge for last. It's a centipede-shaped knoll a half-mile south of the airfield, at the end of a long, furrowed path, poised above a river delta and a blanket of jungle. It was from the jungle that the waves of Japanese assaulted the hill. If they'd taken the airfield, the battle would have turned. The Japanese came up out of the jungle and, for two days, pushed Edson's Raiders back toward the airfield, until just one hill separated the Japanese from the American airplanes: this hill.

Merritt Edson and his Raiders, say all of the books, held the ridge. It is the stuff of marine legend. Colonel Edson was awarded the Congressional Medal of Honor for it, for holding Bloody Ridge.

The books also say that on the second day, at 4 A.M., G Company of the 2-5 was called to back up Edson.

I got an inkling of the gaps in the official history when George MacGillivary had told me, back at the officers' club, "The Second Battalion told the Raiders that they weren't backing up anymore, if you know what I mean. Unless they wanted a bayonet in their back."

"Even though I was not on the Canal," Bill Looney wrote me, "I had heard about Tom and G-2-5 at Edson's Ridge."

"G didn't get the credit it was due in history," Sam Bair told me when I asked him about the ridge. "If it hadn't been for us moving up in the middle of the night . . . we would have lost that ridge. G did a whole lot more than they were given credit for."

Sam Bair's memories of the ridge end with the explosion of a Japanese grenade.

"The two guys in front of me got killed," he said. "I got shrapnel in the legs. It blew me down into the high grass. I just stayed there and got up in the morning, crawled right up out of there. I remember during the night, there was a guy who was wounded in the butt. He kept hollering for the corpsman; every time he cried out, the Japs would run up and stick a bayonet in him. If he'd kept his mouth shut, he'd have been all right."

"We got up there late in the night," Francis Liebermann told me. "The place was just buzzing with Japs and fire and everything else. Edson was right there, helping direct artillery fire—'Bring it in! Bring it in! Bring it in!'—and that saved a lot of things. We backed up the raiders until they got pushed over, and then we became the line. We lost a lot of guys there. I remember one guy, right on the end of our line: Raymond Fryburger, Jr. He was just a young kid, but boy he was mean in a fight. He was practically holding down one end of this line with grenades and a BAR. They said, 'We're going to have to pull back,' and he said, 'Just bring me some grenades and some ammunition. I'm going to stay.' And he did. And he was killed."

And my father?

"He was all over the place. Just like he always was. He had a horseshoe in his pocket."

At first I thought Liebermann meant it literally. But what he meant was that my father was lucky.

"He was in a lot of places he shouldn't have been as a company commander. The guys loved him for it. Everybody did. See, that was the eternal situation: they'd say that if you're up front, you can't see what's going on, so if you're commanding, you should stay back. But he wasn't that way. He was out there in a lot of our firefights.

"Goddamn, we lost all of our lieutenants, and a lot of our NCOs, but the guys always said, 'Tom's got a horseshoe up his ass—he'll go until he drops. He doesn't look like he's going to get it.' "

George Hadzidakis came up the next morning.

"I remember the line where your dad and Edson were," Hadzidakis told me. "We got up there in the morning. I remember that there weren't a lot of marine bodies. The Nips were out there at random, with their rear ends up.

Then I see on the back slope, the marine bodies were stacked. Like four and four and four and four."

After they took the ridge, the 2-5 dug into foxholes for six days, exposed, in the heat.

"Two boys cracked completely," reads Harry Connor's diary.

"After the first night of the battle," Paul Moore wrote, "the colonel filled all the foxholes with Japanese bodies, as a way of frightening the enemy. By the time we saw them, the bodies had blown up like balloons in the tropical sun. I remember seeing the Colonel [Edson] himself driving his jeep along the ridge, laughing and letting out war whoops, as a bloated Japanese corpse, tied to a long rope, bounced crazily behind."

My father crossing the Matanikau at the sandspit. Crossing the Matanikau inland. Saving Edson's butt on the hill named for Edson. I could tell from talking to his soldiers that my father never hesitated to volunteer the services of G company.

"He was a cocky little bastard—he was fearless," Jim Donahue told me. "He'd do anything. I don't know if he thought things out . . . if there was an order, he just did it. He'd say, 'Let's go—let's get the damned job done and get the hell out of here,' where some of us would . . . think things through.

"He was a good marine," Jim Donahue said.

On the top of the ridge, a single obelisk bears a plaque praising Edson's valor. It makes no mention of the G-2-5.

That night, at dusk, I find myself walking out of town,

on the one main road, and listening to the darkness of the jungle. The night fragrance is thick. There are no sounds. It is a darkness as impenetrable as something solid. I cannot envision lying in its belly and waiting for a firefight.

Just before I enter the airport the next day, I fish in my bag for the shell from the ridge, feel its edges, and hold it to my face. I pick up the scent of cordite. Or maybe it's just corrosion. I heft the shell. Then I toss it back into the jungle, where it belongs.

"Gettin' dark now," is how my father's letter ends.

"Let's have the good news. Anything at all.

"It is gettin' dark. Mosquitoes getting to work, bugs chirpin.'

"Love, Tom."

PART II
New Britain

LOOKING BACK, I marvel at the improbable odds against it; I'll never win a lottery at 10 million to one, so why should I lose one? How do you lose a father to a lottery? But when you're a little kid, you don't have the sense to anguish over the illogic of it all; you just watch. I watched the parade of neighbors into our home, people I'd never seen in our house before, with their lasagnas and chicken casseroles and the Rice Krispies marshmallow cakes that my brother and I ate in bed as we watched TV through the afternoons. At night men would come to convey condolences, to see if there was anything they could do. They drank the bourbon he'd bought. I was impressed by the size of the crowd. By the time I was allowed to return to my first-grade class, I felt a certain amount of pride over the magnitude of the thing.

Today the deaths of 134 people in an air crash is tragic, but it's not outside the realm of the conceivable. At Christmas of 1960, though, at the dawn of the commercial jet age, it was as though two comets had collided in the sky. The Second World War, and its lesson that American deaths on a large scale could follow from gallantry and sacrifice, had ended just fifteen years earlier, and we weren't yet accustomed to the idea of random senseless acts of violence. One life lost was still a stunning thing in 1960, even in New York.

The report from the National Transportation Safety Board blamed faulty equipment on the jet, the casual navigational performance of the pilots, and a human snafu in the air-traffic-control system—three derelictions of duty, then, if you count the people who manufactured the mechanical device.

My father's jet was a Douglas DC-8, the most modern aircraft being used in the commercial fleets. As it approached the eastern seaboard from Chicago, the air-traffic controllers gave it a new routing, and while the pilots took note of the route change, one of their onboard navigational devices wasn't working. When they thought they were approaching a key navigational checkpoint in Pennsylvania, they had in fact gone far beyond it.

But air-traffic control in the New York area did not take note of the overflight because it had happened right at a point when the air-traffic controller in charge of one section of airspace was supposed to be handing off the plane to another. The first never confirmed that the transfer had been accomplished, so no one noticed anything until my father's jet, miles off course and going several hundred miles an hour faster than it was supposed to, plowed into a TWA Lockheed Super Constellation, a four-engine prop plane, from the right and the rear. The outer half of the right wing and one of its two jet engines hit the Constellation in the middle of the prop plane's fuselage. The TWA plane went down immediately, onto Staten Island. Among the wreckage was the United jet engine, which had pieces of TWA passengers in it—a detail that leapt out at me when I read the microfilmed accounts not long ago. It would have been in a headline today; at the time, it was buried deep in the story.

My father's jet, missing half of its right wing, limped along for eight miles and crashed into a heavily populated neighborhood in Park Slope, landing on the Pillar of Fire Church. The flames from the crash ignited a seven-alarm fire that destroyed ten brownstones, several shops, and a funeral home. The evening news that night featured pictures of wrapped Christmas presents that had dropped from the sky. The only survivor from my father's plane was Steven Baltz, an eleven-year-old boy from Willamette, Illinois, who was thrown from the tail section into a snow bank, his clothes aflame. He was flying to New York to meet his mother and sister. He was sent to Methodist Hospital, where he died the next afternoon. Before he died, he told a reporter that the city of New York, covered with snow, seen from above as the plane descended, looked like a city in a fairytale.

It had been snowing all morning, the morning of December 16. "I hope your father's all right," my mother had said while my brother and I ate breakfast, and I remember her saying it clearly; I am certain that those were her exact words. She had her back to us, and she was at the sink.

For some reason my brother's fifth-grade class was meeting, but my own second-grade class was canceled. At some point in the early afternoon, with the snow blanketing the yard and coating the rhododendrons, my mother was upstairs taking a nap. I saw a car pull up to the front, a car I didn't recognize. Two men in winter dress coats stepped out, and then one of them helped Emma, my father's secretary, out of the car. The three of them walked up the snow-covered walk, with Emma in the middle, and Emma's expression told me what had happened. I opened the big thick front door before they could hit the knocker, and looked up into Emma's face. She said, "Is your mother home?" and I said, "Is he in the hospital?" She shook her head.

I don't remember going up after them. I do remember that as soon as my brother came home from school, I ran to him and said, "Dad's dead."

In a psychology course at college, several years later, I was the only student in a class of one hundred people who had a memory from the first year of his life, but it didn't surprise me; the day my father died, it was as if the memories of everything that had happened to me in the first seven years of my life were frozen in place by the trauma, like figures caught in the lava of an eruption, or the X-rayed people caught in the blast at Hiroshima. If I was going to be deprived of a father at the age of seven, I guess, I was going to be granted a crystal recollection of all of the moments that he and I had shared together.

I remember the scent of his hair the night I followed him up to their bedroom after he came home from work and changed out of his suit and put on a tweed jacket and hoisted me onto his shoulders and carried me down the stairs. "Watch your head," he said as we started down the stairway, so I buried my face in his hair, dark and curly and thick, just in time to keep from hitting my own head on the ceiling above the stairway. I can still summon that scent whenever I want to.

A moment later, we were sitting at the kitchen table, he flicking peanuts into the air with his thumb and forefinger and catching them in his mouth, me watching him in glee. The rest of the house beckoned beyond the kitchen doors, empty, silent, dark, and secure in a solid suburban way— the earthen, ashy fragrance of the fireplace in the darkened living room, the comfortable sofas and chairs. But it was in the kitchen—well-lit, in the back of the house, away from the street—that he seemed most at home, as if he hadn't bought wholesale into the Bronxville life that the living room represented.

I have distinct memories of everything that happened after his death, too: the flash of the crash froze my future as well. In that case it wasn't being offered in compensation; it was more that the moment he died, I immediately grew up. I was never a kid again as far as I can tell, although I was never really much of an adult, either—lacking someone to show me how to be one, exactly, and rebelling against anything and everything with a periodic reflex. For years afterward I would look around at all the kids I was with in school and wonder why they seemed so blithe, and why they didn't understand the way things are.

"I got a call from Emma," Jim Miner told me not long ago. "She'd talked with the plant manager at the Chicago facility, and he was worried that Tom might have been on the plane."

Jim was talking about the crash, although I hadn't asked him about it.

"I called his dentist. He said he'd arrange to have a dental chart left at the Yale Club. I picked it up and took off for Brooklyn. Because of the chart, Tom was the third person to be identified. The first two were the sanitation workers who'd been crushed on the street in Brooklyn."

We'd been talking about the Boy Scout camp he and my father had gone to, and then suddenly Jim was talking about the day of the crash. I don't know whether it's like this with all people who know someone who was killed in a plane crash—that they never forget its details. I do know that it's a peculiar category of death, that it holds a particular place in the imagination.

Not long ago I read in a newspaper about a professional basketball player who tore up his knee in practice one day. His wife said to their small son, "Dad's been in a terrible accident," and the little boy said, "Was he in a plane crash?"

"I went to Bronxville," Jim Miner told me. "The family had gathered. His mother came over and asked me one question: Did he suffer? 'No,' I said. 'It was instantaneous.' "

Two things about Jim's story rang false to me. One was that it couldn't have been instantaneous. The plane limped along for a full eight miles, crippled, probably traveling under two hundred miles an hour, which gave him a minute or two alive in the plane. This meant that he had a minute or two to contemplate his death as the jet descended with half of a wing missing.

I'm not sure it was as terrible as I've always figured it must have been. As a marine officer, he'd had to contemplate the possibility of death every day for three years. He must have always had it in the back of his head that it might not be instantaneous, and if it were not going to be quick—if he were to die of a wound like Paul Moore's, as he lay in a jungle, bleeding to death—he would know in the last moments of his life that he had died for a good cause.

In the United jet, while it's possible that he knew he was about to die for no reason, it's also possible that he figured he wasn't going to die at all. He'd spent three years in hopeless situations, with a horseshoe in his back pocket. Perhaps he spent his final minute thinking about what to do as soon as the plane crashed, to help the other passengers.

When it happened, my mother told me that he didn't suffer; he always slept on planes, he was probably asleep, and had died instantly. I didn't allow myself to think otherwise until not very long ago. But now I believe that even if he was afraid as the crippled jet swooned its way toward the heart of his city, he pushed the fear to the place he'd pushed it fifteen years earlier in the South Pacific.

I have tried to console myself with the knowledge that he died young and healthy and happy. I would like to think that he was able to say to himself that he was done on earth, and ready to go out. On the other hand, whenever I think about what it is he must have been feeling in those last two minutes, the closer I get to the thought, the more I recoil, and I can never allow myself to try to imagine it fully.

The second thing that rang wrong was Miner's story of the identification of my father's body, because I'd already heard a different version. Bill Looney had written me a letter; he was a company commander in the Fifth Marines under my father's command on the island of New Britain, in January 1944. Bill Looney later worked for United Airlines, and he was part of their accident investigation team;

he was flown in from Chicago and went to the Kings County morgue, where the immediate priority was to identify the bodies.

"There we were at the world's largest morgue," Looney told me. "There were people milling all over the place. Firemen, policemen, hangers-on. The doctor said, 'Keep your eyes open until we can get this place cleared out.' I was wandering around watching over people's shoulders at what they were doing. They'd pull out one of these drawers. Suddenly I noticed your father's neck. I couldn't see anything else. He was upside down. I saw this short, thick neck. I thought to myself, 'My God—that's Tom Richmond.' Just something about the neck and part of his head. I told this to the doctor. I said, 'I've just seen one I can make a positive ID on—a man I thought the world of.' When things calmed down a couple of hours later, I asked the doctor, 'Let's check that.' He pulled the thing out. 'Is that your friend?' he said. 'Sure is,' I said. I don't know where they'd found him."

I asked him how he looked, and Looney didn't hesitate, as he might have if he'd had to put together a lie to protect my feelings.

"He looked pretty good. I couldn't see his face. His body was in one piece. Not burned. Nothing too serious. I've seen it all from the top to the bottom in accidents. Tom, bodily, was in pretty good shape.

"I can still see your dad," Looney told me. "I can still see the part of the neck I was referring to. It was something to me."

Looney had been under my father's command in the battle for Natamo Point on New Britain.

"He was a soldier, boy," Bill Looney told me. "He was a courageous person. To me he had the whole thing. You know, everybody's figure of a marine major is people shouting at people. He didn't have to. He was nice and calm. Just himself. If he told you to do something, you knew you had to do it."

It was at Natamo Point that my father earned his Silver Star, on a spit of land poking out of the densest jungle on the planet. "It was a world-class jungle," Bill Looney told me. "There was no beach. Just jungle. It was so thick it was unbelievable.

"It was more than you could stand."

The island of New Britain, 250 miles long and shaped like a crescent lying on its back, lies east of the mainland of Papua New Guinea, itself one of the most sparsely populated countries on the globe. PNG makes up the eastern half of New Guinea, a large land mass nine hundred miles long and four hundred miles wide, shaped something like an ostrich in stride, one hundred miles north of Australia. The western half of New Guinea is an Indonesian province called Irian Jaya.

New Britain, now divided into the PNG provinces called East and West New Britain, was named by the English pirate and explorer William Dampier in 1700, but no one bothered to claim the place until 1880, when Germany, interested in the copra crops, planted its flag on the island and established German New Guinea. The capital was established at the far eastern tip of the island, in Rabaul, a town surrounded by active volcanoes, located on a large harbor that is the crater of a huge prehistoric volcano.

The Australians took the island at the start of the First World War, solely to capture the Germans' radio base; they allowed the Germans to keep running the plantations. The

Japanese took Rabaul in January 1941, with no resistance; they built a major naval and air base in the harbor to support their southeast expansion into the Solomons.

The emperor's troops didn't give much thought to the western end of New Britain until the allies started marching up the east coast of mainland Papua New Guinea, a hundred miles away across the channel, at which point the Japanese set about fortifying western New Britain. They built a bomber strip at the remote village of Cape Gloucester and launched boat strikes from a peninsula some twenty kilometers west—Natamo Point.

The allies were marching up the New Guinea mainland because Douglas MacArthur had vowed to return to the Philippines, and he wanted help on his flank, and he wanted it from the First Marines. At a meeting of the Joint Chiefs, while the First Marine Division was recuperating from Guadalcanal in Australia, MacArthur had asked for and been given the First Marine Division, sort of on loan. The First Marine Division of the United States Navy's Fleet Marine Force was told, by the commander of the Army, that the island of New Britain was the next stop on its march through the Pacific.

The Japanese had gathered some 10,000 troops on the eastern half of New Britain by the end of 1943, when Radio Tokyo announced to its listeners one evening that because of their "disgraceful conduct" on leave in Australia, the First Marine Division had been summoned again to action. "The First American Marine Division, assorted cutthroats, degenerates, and jailbirds, has been chased out of Melbourne, is now in camp in New Guinea, and will try to invade Cape Gloucester," said the disembodied voice. "I am pleased to add that our soldiers are fully prepared to repulse this insolent attempt. The jungles will run red with the blood of the Guadalcanal butchers."

The division's furlough in Melbourne was eventually tabbed, by someone with a wry sense of humor, the "battle of Melbourne." In the middle of 1943, Australia's young men were off serving the queen in Burma and China and India and North Africa, so that when 10,000 young Americans landed on Australia after defeating the Japanese at Guadalcanal, they were not only welcomed as heroes and given the run of the nation, they were welcomed as healthy young men who hadn't seen white women since leaving Wellington six months earlier.

I heard many rumors about the battle of Melbourne, and some of them had to be grounded in fact. My mother told me that my father professed to having three different girlfriends in Australia, each for a particular reason. One, apparently, gained his favor because her mother could bake good cakes. A second was good at other things, which my mother preferred not to discuss. But she did tell me that soon after they'd been married in 1947, my father had telephoned from the office to ask if he could bring a friend home for dinner, and the friend turned out to be a very attractive blond Australian woman who said over dinner that she'd had many marine friends during the bat-tle of Melbourne, and that she'd decided to travel to the States to find one to marry her—whereupon she produced a list on a piece of paper, at the top of which was my father's name. She crossed it out and, soon after dinner, went about looking for her second choice.

In Australia the division had obviously reveled in pleasure. I came across a lost packet of photographs in an envelope labeled RICHMOND FAMILY TRIP TO ENGLAND, PARIS AND HOLLAND, 1929. But inside were snapshots from Melbourne in 1943. In the first, a gorgeous blonde-haired woman poses behind a white fur, and the inscription reads, "To Tom: with love, Marjorie." A black and white snapshot of a woman who looks remarkably like Ingrid Bergman is inscribed "With best wishes, Eva." A third shows my father with his arms around two other women, and a fourth shows another marine posing for my father's camera hugging two more women.

But according to his records, my father spent more time in Australia in the hospital than outside of it, because he had contracted a particularly virulent strain of malaria on Guadalcanal, courtesy of the mosquitoes that swarmed all over the Matanikau. It was in Australia that my father was promoted, at the age of twenty-seven, to major, prompting a story in the *New York World Telegram* that featured the headline DARTMOUTH CLUB HAILS MAJOR RICHMOND, '38: "There was rejoicing today at The Dartmouth College Club over the news that Harold Thomas Almond Richmond has been promoted to the rank of major at the age of 27. Major Richmond has made the extraordinary record of advancing a grade a year or more since he has been in the marines. . . .

"Classmates recalled that at Dartmouth Major Richmond was a leader in outdoor recreation. He was a member of the Ledyard Canoe Club and of the Cabin and Trail Club that went fishing and hunting in the Dartmouth College Grant forest."

The enterprising reporter had even gone so far as to call my father's home to get some reaction to the happy news, which led to this curious entry: " 'You'd think from reading his letters ever since he left home that he was on a vacation trip,' a member of the Richmond household said today."

Following the battle of Melbourne, the First Division prepared for the invasion by staging drills in Milne Bay, on the southeastern tip of mainland Papua New Guinea. There was nothing to distinguish Milne Bay but jungle and beach. Some of my father's men recall the boredom of the drills. Some of them recall my father's snakes.

"When we left Guadalcanal," Eddie Bryan told me, "he put a snake in his seabag. We didn't see our gear for a couple of months. When he got the bag in Australia, there was the snake. None the worse for wear."

I called J. B. Doyle, one of my father's lieutenants, who said he'd like to talk at length when he was better; he was recovering from cancer surgery a few months earlier, and the therapy, he said, was taking him backwards. I apologized, and offered to let him go.

But he wanted to tell me one thing, he said.

"We bunked together. I'd wake up in the middle of the night and a couple of his snakes would always be on the damned bed.

"He kept me hopping," J. B. Doyle said.

"We shared a tent at Milne Bay," said Jim Tredup. "Those damned lizards and iguanas were always running through the tent. Tom was the only one who wouldn't panic. Particularly on Milne, where they had the coral snake. I lifted up my bag one day and there was a coral snake. I said, 'To hell with that,' and let him keep the bag. Your father was the only one who wasn't scared of them."

"One night," Leonard Lawton told me, "he had a dead snake that he kind of rigged up to scare somebody. He rigged it so they had to reach across it to turn a lamp on in the tent. So the guy turns on the lamp and there's a snake under his arm. Of course, he didn't know it was dead."

Henry Stankus told me about the day they were demonstrating a new explosive on Milne Bay—a land torpedo, a cylinder packed with TNT to be ignited and shoved into a cave—when someone killed a snake. My father was notified, and ended up giving a lecture on the physiognomy of this particular species. Harry Stankus also sent me several snapshots of the weekend he spent with my father and some friends at the farm after the war. In one, Stankus, grinning and holding a can of Schlitz, is watching a friend of my father's sharpen a machete on a large grindstone. In another, three men are loading pistols out in a field of scrub.

"Yeah, for the heck of it I brought up two of my brother's .22 target pistols," Henry Stankus told me. "Tom was horrified. He said, 'Don't shoot any snakes around here.' "

The earliest reference to his infatuation with reptiles—odd when you consider that he grew up in a county adjacent to New York City—occurs in an interview his mother Rebecca Richmond gave in August 1960, four months before my father's death, to the *Chautauquan Daily*. The *Daily* was the newspaper of the Chautauqua Institution, a colony founded in western New York in 1874 for those who wished to appreciate and celebrate the arts. With an amphitheater, a hotel and a "hall of philosophy," it had welcomed noted lecturers and musicians for three-quarters of a century by the time my grandmother was the subject of an article entitled "Rebecca Richmond Is Beloved Writer of Chautauqua Scene."

Rebecca Richmond had been coming to Chautauqua since she was a child growing up in Warren, Pennsylvania, and when she married my grandfather, the two of them spent their summers at the institute, first in the hotel, and then in a house they had built. She wrote a couple of books about Chautauqua, as well as a book of poetry. In the newspaper article she talks of her early summers with her three sons at the colony. Her oldest, she said, was drawn to the music—my uncle Henry. Her second son, she said, had a mechanical bent, and was drawn to the boathouse —my uncle Bob.

"Our third son," Rebecca told the interviewer, "found a friend who liked reptiles as much as he did. They would go hunting for snakes and so forth, which he sometimes kept in his room. Other people got to know about this interest and would bring him additional specimens. One night before we were leaving someone brought Tom a turtle. We didn't know what to do with it, so we left it in the bathtub while we went down for supper. When we came back upstairs we discovered that the turtle had laid an egg in the bathtub."

In fact, the friend in question told me seventy years later, he didn't like snakes as much as my father did. He was just going along with my father's interest.

"We caught our first snake at the assembly grounds at Chautauqua," Ted Gerwig told me. "We found them all over. Ringnecks. Little ones. About a foot long. They bite but they can't kill you. Tom had 'em. I didn't have them. Tom handled them much better than I could handle 'em. . . . He'd collect snakes all over western New York and northern Pennsylvania. We had a whole collection. We kept them in the bathtub. In the hotel."

Gerwig and my father would eventually share an apartment in Manhattan in the late 1930s, after my father had graduated from Dartmouth. While Gerwig was at medical school up at Columbia, he recalls, my father was studying with a herpetologist at the Museum of Natural History, and keeping snakes in the apartment.

Gerwig practiced medicine until a couple of years ago. I asked Ted if he had any idea what it was that attracted my father to snakes.

"I think it was because they were a little risky," he told me. "I think he liked them because there was always the chance you'd get bit."

When I first found Ted Gerwig on the telephone and identified myself, he began to cry. He'd just been watching a documentary on Guadalcanal on television, he told me, and had searched the screen for two hours in hopes of seeing my father's face.

Harry Darrow met my father in the late thirties when they were both young men studying in the herpetology department of the Museum of Natural History. Darrow lived in Mount Vernon, a town adjacent to Yonkers, the home of the Richmond family seat—five acres on a hilltop, a grand old house whose expansive grounds were the stuff of legend for the men who roamed them sixty years ago. Harry Darrow particularly appreciated the expanse of woods behind the Richmond family home, where he would sneak off to neck with his girlfriends.

"Your father used to threaten me—'I'm going to put a spotlight out there, Darrow,' " Harry told me one afternoon. We were standing on the porch of the Richmond home. I had never seen it. It was, indeed, a grand manse once, perched on a hillside, but its stone-walled porch furnished a view of nothing but the roofs of other homes now. The house has fallen into disrepair; it's been chopped up into apartment units. Several cats guarded its arched entrance when we drove up, and eyed us suspiciously.

After the war Darrow and my father became snake-collecting buddies, taking frequent forays down to the Pine Barrens in New Jersey, where they'd collect specimens for the Staten Island Zoo by day and drink in roadhouses by night. Darrow recalls my father's reckless driving: "Every time we had a meeting at the zoo, your father would show up and we'd say, 'Which fender did you wreck this time?' "

Like most of the men who knew him, Harry Darrow does not remember my father being particularly talkative. He told me my father never talked about the war. Then, Darrow said, neither did he. The two of them had an understanding, he said, an understanding shared by the men who'd seen combat, who knew that no one else could comprehend.

"It was as if when you came home," Harry told me, "a curtain had fallen between you and the rest of the world."

There must have been moments when my father, already clearly at home in the wilderness, actually enjoyed his second Pacific campaign; the island of New Britain was nothing but a dollop of solid jungle, which, along with the malaria, the active volcanoes on both ends of the island, and the surreal climate, explained why no European country bothered to claim the island for two hundred years after it was discovered. The marines liked to say of New Britain that in the wet season it rained all day, every day, whereas in the dry season it only rained every day.

On the day of the invasion—December 26, 1943—the first storm struck—"A solid wall of water," wrote Frank Hough in the U.S. Marine monograph. "It lasted for hours. The wind roared in from the Bismarck Sea at hurricane velocity, bringing down giant trees with rending, splintering crashes."

The marines quickly realized that the true opponent on the New Britain campaign would be the elements. The water and the mud jammed their rifles. Nine inches of rain fell in one day. Rain filled up the foxholes. According to the official marine account of the battle, one marine found a nine-foot python in his foxhole during an air raid.

My father's kind of war.

Reaching Natamo Point was not going to be as easy as getting to the mouth of the Matanikau. In fact, up to the moment I left to return to the South Pacific a second time, I had no idea whether I'd be able to find Natamo Point at all. According to various maps, it appeared to lie fifteen kilometers east of the Cape Gloucester airstrip, at the western tip of New Britain. I'd found a travel agent who knew of a puddle-jumping airline to get me to the airstrip, but no one I'd spoken to seemed to know why there'd be an airstrip at Gloucester in the first place. It was the remotest point in the remotest province of the remotest nation on my globe.

But as I waited in the departure lounge at Kennedy for the flight to Los Angeles—then to Honolulu, the Philippines, mainland Papua New Guinea, a place called Hoskins in West New Britain, and finally to Gloucester's airstrip itself—I was oddly unworried about the uncertainty of my plans.

In fact, this time—my second voyage in two years to the underside of the other side of the planet—I felt almost giddy at the open-endedness and endlessness of the voyage. I faced the prospect of cramped economy-class quarters and days without sleep, and aircraft undoubtedly operated by pilots of less than stellar repute, but I was eager to return to the exoticness of Melanesia—an unusual feeling, because until I'd begun this quest, I'd spent my whole life close to home, exploring America.

Snapshots I've dug up through the years show my father as a young teenager on a European tour in the late 1920s—Mont-Saint-Michel, lakes in Switzerland—but thereafter I know of no trips he took to Europe. The proprietor of a paper-bag-manufacturing factory would naturally have spent large chunks of the year on the American road. The gifts he'd bring home from business trips always resonated of distant American cities—saltwater taffy from Salt Lake City, for instance. Salt Lake City sounded like the most exotic place in the world. It was ten years after his death that I first saw the place, after I'd been arrested on its outskirts by the highway patrol for hitchhiking—one of a couple of adolescent cross-country hitchhiking voyages. Thereafter, as a sportswriter for the next twenty years, I traveled through every state, hit every major city, drove most of the highways on the national map and rode every route Amtrak ever invented. I'm a junkie for America.

But this time, to my surprise, I felt the pull of the south-west quadrant of the globe, of the bottomless blue void of the empty reaches of the South Pacific, with its wooden airports, its hand-written receipts, and its out-of-time way of life, in which people moved at a pace that made sense to me. I was hoping to go back in time, much as he had when he was drawn to the farm. I felt the pull all the more strongly in the Kennedy waiting lounge, when I looked up from my newspaper to see a white-faced kid with a goatee wearing a black baseball cap that read NO FEAR—a newly fashionable sporting-goods line, and a faux-fashionable sentiment that struck me that Sunday afternoon as the height of hypocrisy. To me, he looked like the embodiment of fear. Fear of having nothing to do. Fear of having absolutely no idea of what he was doing—now, later, ever. I tried to picture him sitting in a shell hole in the jungle, listening to the whistle of a Japanese 16-inch shell as it whined its way through the pitch dark, wondering if it was going to land fifty yards away, or six feet away, or in his lap. I wondered if he'd be wearing the cap if he were on the docks in Norfolk, Virginia, with a couple of thousand fellow Gen-Xers, waiting to ship out to a jungle in a country he'd never heard of.

Part of me was eager—I couldn't deny it—to play at going to war. I hadn't admitted the peculiar thrill I felt at finding the wreckage on Guadalcanal; now I wondered what kind I'd find in PNG, hoping that the more I found the closer I'd get to his heroism. Just as I'd done with my best friend playing war games in Bronxville after he died. The childhood capacity for delight in war is a deep thing —coded, I'm sure, as deep as any of our genetic cues can be—and entirely free of moral judgment. Back then our games were adventure, pure and simple, and as I boarded the first leg, it occurred to me that the same could be said of what I was doing now. But this was real adventure. I'd had a taste on Guadalcanal, but there'd been something of a theme-park feel to it; after all, I'd procured a war wreckage map from the embassy, and I was making a not uncommon pilgrimage to a famous island. This time my destination was as obscure as the battle that it had hosted.

It took fifteen hours to get to Manila from Los Angeles, with a stop for refueling in Hawaii in the middle of the night. The jet landed in Manila at dawn. My luggage had missed the flight, and wouldn't be delivered for a couple of days. My next flight, to Port Moresby, the capital of Papua New Guinea, was not scheduled to leave until late that evening, so I took a bus into town to buy a new set of clothes.

In the shopping district, next to the Four Seasons Hotel, I found a large department store full of fake Western designer clothes outlets, and bought enough T-shirts and pants and socks to get me through four days of New Britain jungle. When I explained to the teenaged girls behind the cash register that I needed a poncho, they asked what for, and when I told them, they erupted in fits of laughter at the idea of a middle-aged white man foraging in the jungle. They had never heard of Papua New Guinea, which turned out to be seven hours distant on Air Niugini's only wide-bodied jet to Port Moresby—population 170,000, reputed to be something of a cross between Dante's Seventh Circle and the South Bronx. I passed the time in the air reading my tourist guidebook.

"Many people find Moresby a rather dismal place," it explained. "Razor wire, large dogs, and private security guards are everywhere. Be careful. The crime rate is high, and the statistics for rape are particularly bad. If you wouldn't walk around a tough neighborhood in a big city at home, you won't enjoy walking around Moresby. Most residents are as worried about crime as outsiders."

Much of the crime, apparently, is attributable to the use of alcohol. Until 1963 natives were not allowed to consume alcohol; only expatriates could. "It is clear," read my guidebook, "that the effect of beer on PNG has not been a happy one, although you can still walk the streets." (I was to learn, on the day I left the country, that the British government had issued a warning that all citizens of the Commonwealth stay away from Port Moresby.)

The author went on to advise visitors never to go outside after dark. I was not surprised. One of my travel agents advised me to avoid Moresby if at all possible; the Turkish ambassador, he said, had been beaten by a band of rascals —the generic label given to any of the various roving miscreants in the capital city—to within an inch of his life not long ago. Soon afterward, in an extraordinary coincidence, at a party near our home in an extremely rural county of upstate New York, I met an Australian art historian who taught at a college in Brooklyn and had spent several years of his life in Papua New Guinea studying the native theater in the bush. As we left the party, his daughter told me I should look up some of their friends in Port Moresby. They all lived in nice houses behind concrete walls topped by barbed wire. This was mandatory, she said.

We landed in Moresby a few minutes after dawn, after an all-night flight, and as I slumped down the stairway to the tarmac, the heat enveloped me like an old friend; I was back on the equator. The temperature was a given, and thus irrelevant. There was no avoiding it, and so there was no point in worrying about it.

The airport was redolent of the sweat-scent I'd last encountered in the Solomons, and furnished largely in rosewood. Betel juice splattered the floor. I immediately felt something I hadn't anticipated: comfort and nostalgia. It had been more than a year since I'd gone to Guadalcanal, and I felt as if I were back in the fold.

My flight to New Britain did not leave until midafternoon, and it was only seven in the morning. I walked out into the blinding sunlight to find a people-moving vehicle —a PMV—to town. The small buses, I'd read, were routinely held up. My guidebook contained a tourist's first-person account of his PMV being held up by a gang of rascals, who desisted when they realized it wasn't a police vehicle. They'd been waiting to ambush a police vehicle to get revenge on the police who had burned their village in reprisal for their having robbed a PMV.

The winding road to town took us through relatively modern suburbs—small, pastel one-floored cinder-block homes with gardens in which banyan trees grew. A small shopping center anchored each crossroads, usually featuring a cinder-block café offering fish-and-chips and canned groceries. We passed a sign that read COFFINS MADE AND SOLD HERE—BABIES TO ADULTS.

The PMV took us past what was advertised in the guidebook as a beachfront resort: a large hotel built into the side of a hill, largely on concrete planes. According to the newspaper, a local rugby hero had been arrested a few nights earlier for drinking too much in the bar, and smashing some cars in the parking lot. Palms bent to the breeze off the shore, but the breeze carried pieces of paper and plastic along with it. We passed more signs for coffin builders.

In downtown Port Moresby I bought bottled water from Fiji, and the newspapers, which were full of news about the rebels in the far eastern province of Bougainville, and the crime in the city—specifically, the previous day's police raid on the hideout of the nation's most feared fugitive, a man with the evocative name of Leslie Leslie, who had escaped from jail the month before, killed a policeman, and disappeared. Mr. Leslie's apprehension was the latest victory for the police in a losing battle against rampant crime. One newspaper carried a color photograph of the policemen involved in the capture displaying their arsenal: rifles, pistols, and pump shotguns, meant not to impress readers in the way a Western police force might pose for a tabloid, but to instill fear in the anarchic populace. Another newspaper featured a black and white photograph of one of Leslie's confreres. He had been dumped from the police van and lay bleeding for several minutes on the street. The photograph was grotesque, and stunning; it was like a crime photograph from Chicago in the thirties.

There was another story. An Australian man had been shot to death by rascals as he got into his car on a weekday morning to go to work—in front of his nine-year-old son. The men had not been caught.

Back at the airport the sidewalk in front was jammed with Papuans sitting hip to hip, seeking refuge from the midday sun. At the entrance to the terminal, a small snack bar sold ice cream. An entire cone had been spilled, and was slowly melting in a pool. Several people stood around and watched it melt, in disbelief. Their expressions bore the look of people staring at a car wreck.

The island of New Britain comprises two provinces, divided by a straight line right down the middle, like Haiti and the Dominican Republic on the island of Hispaniola. East New Britain is anchored on its far eastern tip by Rabaul, the city of 30,000 whose harbor the Japanese had so coveted. One month before my arrival in Rabaul the volcanoes called Vulcan and Tavurvur had erupted for the first time since 1937. Ash lay three feet thick in some places, and stores and houses collapsed under the weight. A few days later Rabaul police were ordered to shoot looters after one warning.

Nonetheless, East New Britain remains something of a tourist attraction; in my guidebook thirty pages were given over to East New Britain. Three pages were given to West New Britain, my destination, which appeared to be twenty-one thousand square miles of nothing. I was going to a spot on the map called Hoskins. The guidebook did mention the Hoskins Hotel. I'd faxed ahead for reservations, twice, and received no answer.

I was one of a half-dozen passengers on the Air Niugini 737. The Hoskins airstrip was asphalt, and there was a small terminal—a waiting room with several plastic benches, a counter for juice and soda. I asked the man in the ticket agent's office if he could call the hotel for me, and I went to the counter to buy a soda. A barrier of metal bars had been lowered down over the opening, so that the woman selling the food passed me a Coke under the six-inch opening. The barrier seemed incongruous; there was no city here. We were surrounded by woods. But amid all of these trappings of dread, I still felt none.

I returned to the ticket agent's office and asked if he'd called the hotel. "Here he is now," said the ticket agent, and as I turned, the man who greeted me caused a start: whatever it was I had expected, it was not a frail white man whose skin hung on his bones like a suit on a coatrack. After being surrounded for two days by nothing but dark Melanesian faces, I would have been startled by any white face; for a moment I thought that I was overreacting. A grin minus a couple of teeth disarmed me. But Tony Clements's smile was so genuine—he was so pleased to have a guest—that I grew quickly accustomed to his unorthodox appearance. As to the cause of his gauntness, I never inquired. He spoke in a clipped British accent that sounded posh to me.

The Hoskins Hotel lay a half-mile down the road, at an intersection of two roads. This was downtown Hoskins. On one corner stood a store, on another a police station, on a third a giant banyan tree beneath which several dozen villagers lounged. On the fourth corner stood the hotel, a low-slung cinder-block edifice. An antiaircraft gun sat in front of it. No one seemed to notice the gun except me.

It might as well have been guarding the lodge. Clearly the hotel's owner, a Texan who lived in the neighboring town of Kimbe, wanted to seal it off. A chain-link fence had been built across what had once been an open porch, and the entrance to the hotel was now guarded by a locked iron gate over which native sentinels kept a twenty-four-hour vigil.

I was Tony's only guest. In the lobby of the hotel, two natives were knocking down a cinder-block wall, the beginning of a renovation that will likely never be completed. Tony led me to my room. As we walked past the doors to the other rooms, which faced into a grass yard, I was struck by the imaginative decoration on the doors: they looked like abstract paintings of birds of paradise. Closer examination revealed that it was simply brown rubbery latex paint peeled away by humidity thick enough to taste, in random patterns, to reveal the green-yellow paint beneath. The room was made of cinder block; the floor, linoleum laid over concrete. There were clean sheets, and a shower.

I changed my clothes and walked into the dining area where Tony introduced me to Heinz. Heinz was a former soldier in the Australian army, a thick-muscled man with a handsome, hard-set face. He had the gait of an athlete and the paunch of a man who'd spent too much time in the bush with too little to do. This wasn't his fault; Heinz had just joined the staff of the hotel to develop a diving program, but the mysterious American over in Kimbe was not providing the funds at the moment. He hadn't finished preparing Heinz's quarters, or Heinz's dive shop. And Heinz's truck kept breaking down.

It became apparent, here on the fringe, that things happened in fits and starts, and then stopped. Heinz had grown accustomed to it. You don't voluntarily come to PNG expecting things to move from point A to point B. Heinz was living in one of the hotel rooms and waiting for something to happen.

Heinz had quit the Australian army after eleven and a half years. The last few had been spent in PNG as a bomb-disposal expert, taking unexploded shells out of PNG dump sites where the heat of the compost was setting them off, training the PNG Defense Force that has been waging the government's battle on Bougainville for years.

"I spent eleven years doing what everyone wanted me to. Doing what my dad wanted me to. My dad's thing in life was, 'Be a Man! Do something with your life! Join the Army! Make a lot of money, son! Make a lot of money!' " He had been drinking beers; now he was pouring himself glasses of champagne from a bottle he kept beneath the bar. His words were crisp, but his gestures were exaggerated. "Then I realized diving beats working for a living. It's addictive. It's like flying. It's like being Superman. Diving here is the best in the world. The best. The coral, the turtles, the sharks. I said, 'Dad, I will always be provided for. The universe will provide for me.'

"Now, I take trashy dive shops and turn them into fucking phenomenal places. This is my career. I go about it and try to do the best I can."

Over his champagne, and my bottles of SP—South Pacific, the ubiquitous brew—Heinz told me his tales of hand-feeding the sharks off the Great Barrier Reef, and his stint on the Maldives, and his days as a dolphin trainer in the Bahamas. The Canaries. The Caymans. The Swedish girl. The French-Canadian aerobics instructor. It all sounded like Clark Kent making himself out to be immortal and the tales sounded well-worn, lines spoken so often they sounded rehearsed. It was only when Heinz started to talk about his father's exploits in World War II, when he was well into his bottle of champagne, that Heinz's words became more measured, and compelling. His father had been a soldier in the German Army.

"Three and a half years on the Russian front," Heinz told me. "He won the Military Cross. When I get him drunk, he tells me about it."

Behind Heinz glowed a cooler stocked with beer. It was locked. Whenever I asked for another beer, Heinz would unlock the case, give me a bottle of South Pacific, and then lock the case again.

"From what he tells me, when he won the Cross, they were in a village, and they were platoon strength. The machine gun jammed. He's cocking his single-shot rifle, and the guys in front of him are overrun and killed. Finally he gets it going, and fires the machine gun and kills the Russians." Heinz was pantomiming the actions as he described them. War games.

I was ready to sleep for the first time in three days. Heinz told me he'd take me to see a couple of wrecked planes the next morning, before my flight down to Gloucester.

I fell asleep in a minute. In the middle of the night I awoke, and something large was scrabbling on the linoleum floor, or in the wall. Something very large. I figured it was a lizard. My senses heightened, and I listened next for the clatter of reptile feet on the linoleum floor. It didn't come. It came from somewhere inside the wall. I fell back asleep in an instant.

Over breakfast Heinz told me he would take me to the planes if his truck worked and if he could line up a kid for security, to ride figurative shotgun on the pickup.

"We don't go out there," he said, "without a native." Heinz said that he found the natives to be lovely people, as a rule, when they were sober. And as for Heinz, I was amazed to see that he did not appear to be hungover himself.

The guard unlocked the gate to let me out of the hotel. Several of the natives sitting beneath the banyan tree across the road followed my steps with indifferent gazes. The antiaircraft gun was in remarkable shape, virtually intact, right down to the metal seat for the gunner in which a villager sat, chewing betel. He had a feather in his hair. He smiled and moved, to let me sit in the seat.

It had no meaning to me. Amid a hundred villagers, next to a barricaded hotel, the gun had no context. I was reminded of the time my son and I visited the NASA Space Center, with its various attractions—including real space helmets, chained to the wall lest they be stolen. Slipping one over my head, I felt no closer to the stars than if I'd been watching an episode of *Star Trek*. Now, sitting in the Japanese gun, I felt as if I were watching *Bridge over the River Kwai*.

Heinz rounded up a native and drove us down a long dirt road next to the Hoskins airstrip. The native was bouncing along in the bed of the pickup behind us.

"I want to put together a tour," Heinz told me as the pickup waddled down a grass lane toward the jungle. "There's a gorgeous hot springs a few miles away, and I'm talking with the chief of the local tribe."

Heinz had competition. Several kilometers up the road was the Walindi Plantation Resort, near the village of Talasea—an expensive and well-maintained resort that featured diving. Heinz had to come up with something to lure the divers. He had recently come across the wreckage of two Japanese planes in the jungle next to the airport. There is business in wreckage.

As we tromped through the jungle, I began to feel a familiar sensation—the adrenaline rush I'd felt when Selwyn and Peter and I found the wrecked bomber back on Guadalcanal. It had been nearly a year since I'd walked through a jungle to find a wrecked airplane, but within seconds, as I wound my way down the overgrown trail— several yards ahead of Heinz, like a bloodhound racing ahead of the hunter—the whole sensation came back: the searing heat, but devoid of the white sun, which was trapped in the tree canopy above us; the rotting, verdant undergrowth scent, woody and green, with a fecund feel as if life itself could spring from the rot, the mire of spontaneous generation; the give of the ground, spongy and waiting to trip me.

We hadn't even reached the planes yet when I felt them, and in the back of my mind there was a feeling like a cross between relief and exhilaration. And when I saw the two of them—a Betty and a Zero, bombed on the ground—I felt something else again: the unmistakable sense of the war, the sense that had been missing from the warplanes in the Vilu Village museum back on Guadalcanal. These planes had been waiting by the side of the runway when the Americans had strafed them and bombed them. Vines now gripped the aluminum, and were slowly tugging them apart; it would take decades, or centuries, but eventually the fingers of the vines would tear them apart completely. Perforated by hundreds of bullet holes, they had come to rest where they were supposed to rest, here at the airfield the Japanese had used for their troops in the central part of the island when the marines overran them on their evacuation east across New Britain. And I could feel the war in them. I ran my hands over the aluminum, and ducked beneath the wing to locate the red circle, now faded into light pink, and absently ran my hands over the rivets, and stuck my head into the cockpit of one of them.

We had to get going, Heinz told me. I think he believed a band of rascals was going to come across us, in the jungle. On the drive back to the hotel I found myself telling Heinz how well preserved his planes were. How he could put together a brochure for his prospective clients—talk about how the Americans had bombed the airfield and caught the Japanese sleeping. Brag about the excellent condition of the two planes.

Part of me recoiled at the notion that I was helping him market the death the planes represented. But part of me would do anything to immortalize what the marines had done.

I've always been hooked on the detritus of the past. In the States I spend a lot of time searching out rusted train cars and deserted train stations, or empty office buildings from the thirties, in every town and city I visit. I don't look for restored train engines, or Pullman cars made into restaurants or museums; they feel like nothing to me. It's only when I find a rusting engine on a side track, or a string of old passenger cars—abandoned, windows broken—or a couple of cabooses that I explore them. Actually, I break into them. I always know when I've found what I'm looking for in the trains, if it's there. I can feel it.

I avoid the restored train stations; the secrets they hold have been painted over, prettified, packaged as nostalgia instead of being left to bear witness. But others are abandoned and boarded up, and when I break into them, I feel their life. I've broken into the train stations in South Bend, Indiana, and Kansas City, Missouri, and a dozen small towns. It's a weird habit, I guess; I've never run into anyone else who shared it. But it's easy to explain: it wasn't just the model train set in the basement that imprinted trains on my soul; it was that he rode trains to work every day, from Westchester to Grand Central, and then the subway out to Long Island City. And it wasn't a train that killed him. Trains embodied his age the way jets embody ours, and it makes perfect sense that I would spend my time looking for tangible physical ties to his time. Rotting stations and rusted cabooses are closer to my father's world than restored ones; when I get lucky, and find a place no one has set foot in for half a century, I am as close to his being alive as I can ever get. They are time machines for me.

On the wall in my office at work, next to my computer, I have pinned a black and white photograph, now faded into brown and white, that I found in an antique store in upstate New York. It's a picture of the inside of a lounge car on the Mercury, the New York Central's legendary streamliner between Detroit and Cleveland. The photograph is taken from one end of the car, looking down its length. The plush carpeted aisle is flanked by easy chairs and end tables with lamps on them. The design of the lamps and lampshades is slightly Eurofuturistic; the furniture is most definitely of an era. The lamps appear to be turned on, even though sunlight is coming in through the windows of the car, which is at rest in a station. Halfway down the car a partition features a mural of clouds in the sky. It is called the Cloud Car. All of its chairs are empty, waiting to be filled.

I stare at it for long periods of time. I think that there are people in those chairs, and if I stare long enough, I will find myself in that car, on the other side.

My great-grandfather and his partner founded the Potdevin Machine Company more than a hundred years ago in Brooklyn. They manufactured machines that made paper bags and cardboard boxes. During the 1940s my grandfather and his partner decided to set up their own paper-bag-manufacturing plant. They called it the Custom-Made Paper Bag Company, and they put it in a turn-of-the-century brick factory. Several years after the war my father was chosen to run it. It manufactured ice-cream-bar wrappers. One day I went to the factory with him. We rode the trains together; I can still picture the white tile of the station walls. When we reached the factory, it wasn't the thousands of Good Humor wrappers—Creamsicle wrappers—that I found fascinating, but the sound and bulk and iron feel of the machines that were spitting them out.

Maybe it was these machines that instilled my love of machines—not modern machines, but the machines that operated by physical laws that we could understand. Modern machines are helping us lose touch with how work looks, which is a valuable thing to have and a dangerous thing to lose. The famous Edward Weston photograph of the man turning the gear—a graphic, poignant, and beautiful illustration of one man, with the strength of his back, manipulating a man-made thing and, with its help, levering a change in his environment—would today be a photograph of a man at a keyboard, entirely divorced from the work being done.

Of course I like trains. He didn't die in a train. He died in a plane—going too fast, the technology running ahead of itself. Putting that DC-8 in the hands of that pilot, who had to rely on bad equipment and ground-control error, was proof to a little boy that man had pushed technology beyond its natural station, and that technology had pushed man beyond where he was supposed to go.

"Imagine a black hole. We're at the bottom of it. This is where the world stops," Tony said as if he were proud to be at the bottom of it. We were in his office at the hotel, in November on the equator, listening to Christmas carols on his tape deck. He had taken the tape out of his tape box, and he knew where to find it; it is there for him every autumn. Then again, I thought, perhaps he plays it year-round.

We sat and listened together for a moment. It had been fifty-one years since the marines landed on New Britain the day after Christmas 1943, after eating their last meal of steak and eggs, a dish that would be adopted as the traditional marine landing meal ever after, having been discovered in the battle of Melbourne.

Tony Clements had been a chef. He trained in London as a young man and went to sea with Cunard. *Queen Elizabeth,* from Southampton to New York. There were five kitchens on her. He started cleaning the kitchen and peeling potatoes, worked his way up to chef-to-party. He grew fed up with London. His sister had emigrated to Australia. He followed her. Didn't much care for Sydney. Perth was one big rat race.

"I answered an advert—they wanted a chef for a motel in Rabaul—and it's been PNG ever since."

He has found his place. Not even his mugging could move him off the turf: he pulled from the wooden desk drawer two aging newspaper clippings from 1987, reports from the Port Moresby paper that detailed Tony Clements's savage beating at the hands of some rascals. He had been flown out to the hospital in Sydney, so severe were his wounds. He quickly returned.

"No one can say what draws you back," he says.

The missing teeth make the smile more endearing somehow.

"I'm here because I want to be here. Bit by bit. We'll get there. I've got all the time in the world. I'm here as long as it takes."

I said goodbye. The flight west to Gloucester would be

leaving soon. I walked down the road, alone, encumbered by my pack. Heinz couldn't drive me; the truck was broken. I thought briefly of asking him to walk the mile with me, for fear that the place was as sinister as he'd made it out to be. I didn't. The guard unlocked the gate and let me out one last time, and I was free.

Within a dozen yards I was sweating freely in the noon sun, and as I walked down the road, going against the grain of villagers and natives walking to the market, I must have struck a comical figure: a white man, dressed uncomfortably—in long pants!—laden with luggage, as out of place as a slug on a white linen tablecloth. But I found myself grinning and smiling and nodding "Moneeeen" at everyone, and everyone smiled back. It was then that I turned my back on Heinz and Tony—the two of them, barred against the world; one come to rest, the other restless; both bound by having abandoned any hope of finding what they had set out to find, because neither, like most expats, knew what it is they were looking for in the first place.

Fifty years ago the First Marines had come here to defend what Heinz and Tony had fled: civilization as society. The marines fought to suppress tyranny, to entitle all good men and women to the blessings of freedom and democracy. Then, when the task was done, they returned to their lives back home, their jobs, their suburbs—democracy's illusion of freedom, every man a king, but in fact a style of life in a subset where behavior was strictly prescribed.

If there was a sadness on their faces, on Heinz's hard features and Tony's emaciated ones, it was no different than the sadness of every man unable to fit into his community. These two had made no pretense of trying; they abandoned it. As my father abandoned Bronxville whenever he could, for the farm, an expatriate ill at ease in suburbia.

My oldest brother remembers that my father didn't seem to like his job.

"He hated it," he told me. "I remember growing up, and it was kind of strange because he would be out at the crack of dawn to go to Long Island City and he would be cursing in the morning, in the dark morning; he'd wake me up. He'd be cursing, walking around, and then he'd be gone."

My oldest brother, Lee, is actually my half-brother; his father was my mother's first husband, whom she married in 1941. My brother was one year old when his father went to the Pacific with the Navy, in August 1944. In December, a Kamikaze plane hit his ship, and he died. When my mother married my father in 1947, my father adopted Lee.

I asked him what he remembered about my father at the farm.

"Basically he came back from the war and was handed Custom-Made Paper Bag—and his dad told him, 'Now you're going to be a paper-bag manufacturer.' And because of the intense duty focus of the Richmond family, he did it. But in the same way he was a marine hero, he had to be a paper-bag hero. So he went on and became a paper-bag hero and took it as far as he possibly could."

In addition to being the president of the paper-bag-manufacturing operation, my father was a member of the board of directors of the Potdevin Machine Company, and its president. In the seventies, the Potdevin Machine Company folded the paper-bag-manufacturing operation into their plant in Teterboro, New Jersey. Bob Potdevin, Sr., today the president of the company, and the grandson of the founder, met me for lunch at a restaurant near the plant. He told me that when my father took over the Custom-Made business after the war he made more money out of it than anyone else had. Then he told me about one of dad's business trips out to the Midwest when he would try and drum up business for the Custom-Made Paper Bag Company.

"Of course, those trips would take months," Potdevin told me. "And he had to pick up his snakes wherever he could. We were in Chicago at the Edgewater Beach Hotel. It had this beautiful red carpeting. He lost several snakes. There's this red-carpeted hallway, and these snakes are slithering down the red carpet."

Another time, Bob told me, my father was coming back from a snake-hunting trip in North Carolina with the sales manager. They were pulled over and the trooper asked them to open the trunk. There were money bags in the trunk, but they didn't have money in them. They had rattlers.

"He was a good party man," Potdevin told me. "Once a year he'd throw a big party and all the bankers would come. Well, we always owed the bankers money. One time, at one of many parties, he wiped the bankers out in craps. I was saying to him, 'For God's sake! Stop beating these guys!' But Tom was just raking it in.

"Of course, back then," Bob told me, "the idea was to start drinking on Friday night and be sober for Monday morning."

• • •

I remember the parties more than anything else—the late-night din of a buzzing, smoky crowd drifting up to the top of the stairs, and me descending, four or five years old, curious, thrilled to find so many people having so much fun, my father in the green-leather wingback chair, a glass of bourbon in his hand. I was delighted to be passed around, to be put on display in pajamas, to see the faces of my friends' moms and dads done up in unusual and exotic expressions, the women's lipstick a vivid scarlet, the place fragrant with Kent smoke and Lark smoke and women's perfume. Then, the morning after, I ran the early-morning gauntlet of the living-room furniture en route to the television room: ashtrays piled with lipsticked filters on the table, redolent now not of the excitement of live smoke, but of the dead chemical scent of the cold butts; the glasses scattered on the tabletops, half-filled with light amber liquid, my own head just high enough to catch the curl of its sweetly sickening fragrance sneaking out over the tops of the glasses.

The whole house would be lit by the glow of Saturday-morning winter sun glinting off the snow out in the front yard. All the rooms were light and windowed. All of the rooms were nice, except my father's office, which was on top of the garage, and unheated. It was in his office filing cabinet, my oldest brother told me, that he found the .45 pistol. All I remember about his office was a big wooden desk and an ocarina—his sweet potato. It was made of plastic, white and pink whorls. It had finger holes—a strange flutelike thing. I never heard him play it. I have never seen one since.

In retrospect, I have probably couched the parties in Cheeverish finery, and perhaps confused some details of

121

Bronxville with some of Bullet Park, although I don't remember any outrageous behavior or drunken displays in the real-life version, only warmth and intrigue and the high-colored etch of the women's makeup. Bronxville and Bullet Park had in common names like Gregory and Fletcher and Snyder and Weymouth and Richmond, good Anglo monikers all.

I know it was bourbon because just before my father's death, preparing for the Christmas parties of 1960, he had bought a case of Jack Daniels, and all the men in town knew it, and so there was a disproportionate number of male mourners and comforters among the crowds who showed up with their plates of food after he'd died.

I do know that the cocktail-party memories are as good a measure of his life as any. Otherwise, why would my parents have posed for *Life* magazine's examination of the suburban cocktail party, in which the editors examined this peculiarly fifties phenomenon the way Margaret Mead might have analyzed a bush family? One photo essay in the series depicts a young actor named Tony Randall playing the role of several different cocktail party habitues—the rake, the drunk, the wolf. In the photograph in which my parents appear, which depicts some thirty people in various states of cocktail-party socializing, my father is posed in conversation with a woman, and his is the most uncomfortable expression in the room. I have no doubt that he was wondering what in the hell he was doing posed like some mannequin with a glass of bourbon in his hand when he could have been on the porch at the farm with a glass of bourbon in his hand.

"I always felt personally," my oldest brother told me, "that the farm was the antidote to Custom-Made."

Jim Miner, who had been our family's attorney, told me that something else was involved.

"His father had encouraged him to buy the land after the war," Jim Miner told me. "He was concerned."

Concerned about what?

"Well, your father was one of a host of guys who'd had a tough war."

I have often wondered whether it was the tough war that gave him the temper, or made him want to spend long hours alone in the forest, or drink, or drive maniacally. But for all of the changes I am certain it effected in him—in all of them—I don't think it made him bitter or troubled.

For one thing, I share all of the traits I've just described, in spades. For another, his love of wilderness and solitude is well documented in his childhood and adolescence. The war did nothing to temper his goofy sense of humor—one day, having been growing a mustache for several weeks, he returned from the office with half of it shaved off, and pretended to not know why we were laughing. The men with whom I spoke invariably cited his sense of humor, both during and after the war.

This is not to diminish the truth of Jim Miner's recollection; no doubt, his father had reason to be concerned. No doubt the nature of the trauma was deep. If post-traumatic stress syndrome had not been yet identified, that didn't mean it didn't exist. The nightmares in which my mother heard him shout out the names of his men attest to a postwar stress, but his inability to remember them when he woke also suggests psychological defenses at work, and suggests that those defenses were in play in his waking, later life. The farm surely provided him with a necessary place for escape and release.

I could feel the transition from the suburb to the outback in the back of the station wagon—smooth parkways for the first couple of hours, then more tightly swerving curves on the back roads, and then, finally, the pounding of the chassis on the final few miles of pitted dirt road. The back of the speeding wagon would bounce like a jackhammer and plumes of dust would rise from the back of the car like a smokescreen. Then, finally, we'd pull up next to the porch, its paint invariably flaking, that wrapped around to the side of the house. I'd jump out of the back and sprint down the dirt road, into the cool darkness beneath the trees, and pee into the ferns that grew by the thousands at the side of the road. Then I'd run back to the house and sprint down to the pond to find the salamanders, their smooth, wet green skin speckled by tiny red dots, their lungs pumping in panic behind their impossibly fragile ribcages.

The summers were warm and safe. We were cushioned by hundreds of acres of mysteriously deep woods whose floor was an endless soft carpet of rust-colored pine needles. I'd walk into the darkness of the cave to get away from the heat, and discover mysterious rock walls, or the rusted Model T, whose cracked steering wheel moved a few inches to each side.

When we'd walk down the trail to the pond, he'd stop to look for snakes, and once motioned for me to get down on my hands and knees to look under a scrubby bush. I did, and for a moment I could make out only shadow. Then, as my eyes adjusted, I saw a huge king snake, coiled into a ball, supremely bored.

At the pond there were leeches in the water, but I don't

recall any revulsion when my father or mother or brother had to take them off me, just as I don't recall any fear when my father came out of the woods one day with a snake for me. It was the end of a normal summer day— me playing somewhere out in the warm field grass, the soporific symphony of field insects broken only by the rise and fall of the chainsaw somewhere out in the sea of pines. Only this time he was holding the snake, a fantastically colored thing, gray—silver when I think of it now, the scales of the animal lending a luminescence to the color— dotted by oval spots the color of Georgia clay soil. It was probably no more than a foot in length. He wound it around my right wrist, where it coiled, heavy, and friendly. Then it leaned over and bit the forefinger of my left hand, and left two small pinpricks, and it hardly hurt at all.

"He used to have this little garter snake run over his neck," John Stankus told me. John was Henry Stankus's brother. John Stankus was up there picking blueberries with him one weekend after the war. John had been in my father's company on Guadalcanal before they shifted John over to the 1-5, where he became a regimental scout for the regiment. John Stankus won a Silver Star for the battle of Nameless Hill at Cape Gloucester.

"He liked the well up there," John Stankus told me. "The well up at your country place."

Because the water was so pure?

"Naw, to keep his beer cold," Stankus told me. "He'd take a six-pack and sink it down in the well on a rope. 'That gives it the right temperature,' he'd say. 'I can sit here and drink it all night.'"

John remembers asking my father if he could shoot some

deer with his rifle. My father told him that in Massachusetts you could shoot deer legally with a shotgun, but not with a rifle, and that if he shot them with a rifle, well, he was welcome to, but he was on his own if he got caught.

"I liked Tom," John told me. "He always put his cards on the table."

John remembers the time porcupines ate one of his canoes. They'd kneel down to see the porcupines under the porch: "You'd see the pink eyes shining back at us. But he wouldn't kill them. He was a man all the way through."

It took me a moment to follow John Stankus's train of thought: that my father, in refusing to kill a porcupine, was more of a man for it.

Not long before my father died, on a drive home to Westchester he turned to my mother—I see them as two cameos, facing each other, profiles outlined dark against the Sunday afternoon sunlight in the windshield—and said, "If anything ever happens to me, don't sell the farm." But she did, a couple of years later, because she had no income. She got thirty thousand dollars for the farm from the Girl Scouts of America, who turned it into a summer camp.

My own family lives now in the country—a place not as remote as the farm, but relatively out of the way. It's three and a half miles outside a depressed farm village. We own one-hundredth of my father's acreage, but it's enough. At night there are no sounds. The stream across the road is small, but there's a swimming hole. We're renovating our house. My wife takes on each room as if it's an enemy, and defeats it, so that it is redone. My own office is in a wing off the kitchen. It's pretty raggedy, and it's always cold.

· · ·

At the Hoskins airport, an agent for an airline called Air-link checked my ticket. I turned to the man next to me, and he nodded politely, wearing an expression that revealed nothing. He was shorter than I, and stout, with a bush-man's oval face and beard, and teeth stained red by betel nut. A multicolored billy was slung over his shoulder. Something at rest about him prompted me to ask him if he was going to Gloucester. He said that he was. I told him I was looking for the places where my father fought, and I showed him my official marine book about the battle of New Britain, published soon after the war. He told me that he knew of a house where I could stay in the village.

An old twin-engined Cessna took us over some moun-tains to Gloucester. I sat behind the pilot, a young Austra-lian who kept taking sips of water from a plastic jug that featured a strip of masking tape with his name written on it in smudged pencil: Andrew Talbot.

I took stock of the plane: on the left wing, oil was bub-bling out of the Phillips-head screws that held the cowling on the Titan engine. Cracks scarred the plastic of the win-dows. Plastic was chipping off his steering wheel. The rub-ber sealing between the windows and the metal was rotted. And a warning light on the control panel read LEFT AL-TERNATOR OUT.

"It's the fuse," he told me. "We'll get to it. Not essential. Just happened today."

I was reminded of a day in 1978 when I was covering a minor-league hockey team for the *New Haven Journal-Courier*. I had to fly to Binghamton, New York, because I had missed the team bus. There was a flight on Mohawk Airlines from Kennedy via Westchester County Airport. It was an old two-engine prop plane, its design marking it to be a product of the forties—curving wing surfaces, bulbous engine cowlings. I remember at the time remarking at how old the plane looked; I didn't mind, having always trusted the old over the new anyway.

When the plane landed in Westchester and took on new passengers, I looked up from my seat and felt a painless but physical jolt somewhere in the back of my brain. The man standing in the aisle about ten feet away, with his back to me, was my father. The tweed coat, the haircut, the unmistakable shape of the back of his head. It wasn't someone who, from behind, looked like my father; it *was* my father. I was certain of it. I was so thoroughly disoriented I was way beyond fear; I was simply lost. I actually wondered what I was going to do when he turned around. I had never felt anything like it, and never have since.

When he turned around, it wasn't my father. He didn't look anything like him.

As the plane took off, I couldn't make any sense out of my newspaper. I was literally shaking. I stared out the window. I was sitting over the left wing, which housed one of the prop engines. Some two dozen bolts held the metal cowling on top of the engine. When we took off, one of the loose bolts started to vibrate in its hole. I watched the bolt work its way out, thread by thread, as the wind pulled at it. It looked like a long worm slowly working its way out of a hole. I was frozen. I couldn't take my eyes off it. I figured it would fly out, and if I didn't feel a jolt from the rear of the plane, then everything would be okay. But after five inches of the bolt was exposed, it stopped coming out. It looked as if about one inch of the bolt was still in the hole, and the five inches that were sticking up were heavy enough to lean back in the wind and hook the remaining inch in the hole. And there it stayed, swaying a little from side to side, but not coming out.

If it tore loose, the engine cowling would not come off, but I also knew that a six-inch bolt, tearing into the tail-wing, could sever all the hydraulic mechanisms, and the plane would drop. I considered finding a flight attendant, but it was a small plane, and there was only one attendant, and she was in back. The thrum of the engines made the cabin loud, so I would have had to climb past the man to my right and alert her, and she would come look at it, and that would alarm everyone on the plane, and there was nothing they could do anyway except land the plane, which was going to happen anyway. So I watched the wing until the plane reached Binghamton, and as we started our descent, and the plane slowed, the bolt began to work its way back into the hole, as if the film was being played in reverse. And as we hit the runway, it plopped back into its hole.

As I got off, I told the attendant about the bolt. She thanked me and said they'd look at it. And then, as I walked through the Binghamton airport, my eyes fixed on a small model in the airport terminal, in a plexiglass box, of a modern jet—I think it was a DC-9—and there was a legend next to it that said MOHAWK AIRLINES FLIES DC-9 JETS EXCLUSIVELY. Which, of course, they didn't. Unless they did.

The plane was supposed to go down, and my father's ghost had gotten on at Westchester—either to warn me, or to be with me as it went down, or—and this is my favorite interpretation—to keep the accident from happening.

Today the closest city to our house in the country is Binghamton, and I fly out of the airport several times a year.

• • •

Despite the well-worn features of the Cessna, and the absence of an alternator, the flight to Gloucester was uneventful. We flew over green humps of jungle whose curves began to mesmerize me from above; they looked as if you could dive into their folds. We had one stop at a place called Kandrian. Kandrian's dirt airstrip, on top of a hill, ended with an abrupt cliff, beyond which lay a horizonless ocean, but Andrew Talbot pulled the Cessna to a halt a good hundred yards short of the end of the strip. He parked the plane to unload a hand-pushed lawn mower to a man wearing a T-shirt bearing the legend STATE OF ORIGIN. Lots of people in the South Pacific wear T-shirts and jackets emblazoned with English legends that mean nothing—phrases lifted free of any context. At first I didn't understand it. Now I do. Whenever I yearn for the aimless and timeless nature of life on the islands I visited, I think of T-shirts that mean nothing.

We took off again, and a few minutes later, as I looked down, directly beneath the plane I saw the topography I'd studied for months in new and old maps: Borgen Bay and Natamo Point. I opened the marine monograph on New Britain and compared the aerial photograph in the book to the shore below. It was identical, in a way that I hadn't been prepared for. In Guadalcanal the distinguishing topographic points had been, for the most part, largely overgrown: The mouth of the Matanikau was a settlement: Point Cruz now housed the harbor and the docks. Even Henderson Field was now an international airport with a gas station and rental-car agency across the road.

But the landscape I saw beneath me in Papua New Guinea showed virtually nothing made by man, save a few huts. The shoreline, Yellow Beach in the monograph, was a crescent of black sand and nothing else, as it had been when my father landed on it. Out of the blue I remembered the *Twilight Zone*'s "Odyssey of Flight 33," in which a DC-8 descends from a cloud bank to Manhattan, only to be confronted by nothing but jungle. The sense of time displacement I'd felt in Moresby had been heightened; I was farther back. It was where I wanted to be.

I'd assumed that when we reached the airfield, I'd see signs of civilization; surely a village or town would have sprung up around the airfield. But within a few minutes the airstrip lay beneath us—long, wide, overgrown with parched yellow grass—with nothing around it at all.

As Andrew Talbot came in on his final approach, I saw, alone in the grass a few hundred feet beneath us, the wreckage of a two-engined American fighter plane. The fuselage had plowed into a ridge, and the wing had flown ahead another fifty yards.

Our plane bounced onto the dirt, the little Cessna impossibly tiny to be bouncing down this airstrip built for the likes of B-29s. There was nothing to be seen in any direction. The strip felt like a piece of African veldt. I realized I had stumbled, again, into a remarkable piece of luck: if I hadn't approached the man at the Hoskins airstrip, I'd be landing in the literal middle of nowhere, with nowhere to go. As the Japanese had relinquished the airstrip quickly, so had the Papuans; the village was fifteen kilometers away. A white pickup truck appeared from behind a dry grassy bluff. It was there to pick up my newfound sponsor, whose name, I discovered, was Popsy Sinivei. Popsy motioned for me to get in the cab; I insisted on riding in the bed in back. Popsy shrugged, and rode up front with his friend Charles. Charles was wearing a pair of pants that displayed the word "Final" in various typefaces.

It was very hot and dry. The rains had not yet started. The plane turned around, Andrew floored it, and the Cessna lifted off within a hundred yards, leaving behind an incredible stillness. Behind the airfield rose a series of parched hills, and behind them, a larger hill.

"Volcano," Popsy told me.

The drive to the village was a forty-five-minute odyssey over a dusty pitted road flanked by horned oxen, pigs, and pieces of the war, left exactly as they'd been fifty years earlier. We passed a Sherman tank, and a dozen amtracks. There were no plaques to commemorate anything—not the battle for the airfield, not the battle for Nameless Hill.

Here, for the natives, there was no market in removing the wreckage, or even moving it. No one collected it because no one had any real idea of what had happened here. In West New Britain, fifty is old.

The fiftieth anniversary of the landing on New Britain was one month away, but no marine alumni would return. No one much cares to remember a battle in which the jungle was the chief enemy. The wreckage lay where it had died. It had taken on the patina of the jungle, and it looked as if it belonged. I was eager to find it.

We pulled into a fenced-off area just south of the village, with four houses in it that comprised the government compound built by the Australian International Development Assistance Bureau—AIDAB. A joint venture between Papua New Guinea and Australia, AIDAB was modernizing two rural outposts in the entire province: Kandrian and Gloucester. All four of the houses, like the huts in the rest of the village, were built on stilts, suspicious of the tides; the ocean lay just a few yards away.

As Charles pulled the pickup into the bay beneath Popsy's house, an ominous metal grinding sound issued from the chassis. The expanse of grass between the houses was marked by two circles, ten feet in diameter, in which the grass was a lighter color: bomb craters. On the circumference of one Popsy's wife had planted flowers. A large green parrot floated from one tree to another. Popsy explained that I could stay in the house belonging to an AIDAB volunteer from Australia who was off in Kimbe. I'd have electricity for six hours a day, and plumbing. First Marine Division luck. A man appeared with a toolbox and began to take the differential apart. I took stock of the topography, and realized that the compound lay at the foot of Target Hill, next to Yellow Beach on Borgen Bay—where my father had landed. A few hundred yards from Natamo Point. I'd come halfway around the world, to one of the most sparsely populated countries on the planet, with absolutely no advance planning, and found a house to stay in, for free, exactly where my father had fought and had won his highest decoration.

"Mud and rain. Mud and rain. That was it," Frank Bacon told me: Bacon was a platoon leader in the First Battalion of the Fifth Marines. He wanted to talk about the weather and the terrain, as they all did. The fighting was obviously secondary; fewer than 400 marines lost their life in the New Britain campaign, but none of the survivors considered it an easy fight. They loathed it.

"We were the army by that time, of course, so we had gotten army equipment, and one of the things they had was this nice little jungle hammock," Bacon said. "Lightweight. A tarp to give you shelter, mosquito netting. You'd sling it between two trees. Well, you'd wake up in the morning and reach down for your boots, and all you'd find was water."

The marines took to cutting holes in the bottom of the hammocks so the water could run out. It didn't do any good.

"The first night," recalls Jay Henry Gustafson, a company commander in the 1-5, "we were asked to move up in the middle of the night, wading in knee-deep and waist-deep water, and you couldn't see. We were most ineffective."

Troops never dried out during the entire operation. Falling trees killed nearly 20 marines. Patrols in the rain went around in circles. Friendly fire marked the first few days of fighting.

"It was almost hard to believe that there was so much rain," Bill Looney told me. "I believe we heard there was over three hundred inches a year. Somewhere along the line I looked that up. It was an impossibility to stay dry no matter what you did. Just remarkable. You were constantly wet because no matter what happened, the foliage would still be wet from the day before. It was hilly. There were no places to walk. There weren't a whole lot of trails. We had a storm at one time that was so heavy you had to stand some place just huddled together. One time we were on a patrol. When we got back, we found out we'd lost our post office—everything: the whole kit and caboodle just floated away. It was just washed away. With all the mail to be passed out."

They'd landed on the day after Christmas, to no opposition. The first concerted fighting occurred around the airfield. It's indicative of the place history would assign the campaign that the first battle of any note was called the

134

battle of Nameless Hill. On the second day on the island, the 1-5—1,000 men—went up into the hills behind the airfield and disappeared. Radio contact was lost. The regiment sent John Stankus out to find them.

"I took a kid with me to be my runner and left the airstrip, just breaking daylight, and started up the other side," John Stankus told me. "It's just light enough to see things when I come up this grassy knoll and I see a half-dozen Japs. They were just getting up. They started at me.

"I said to my runner, 'Kid, run back as fast you can or I'll run your ass over.' He kept wanting to look over his shoulder. 'Don't look back!' I said. We ran as fast as we could. When we got back, I told the colonel the Japs had moved back in during the night."

The colonel told John to go find his brother Henry, the company commander of the F (Fox)-2-5, and point him toward the enemy.

"So I go down to Fox," John said, "and my brother says, 'Yeah, that's our guys. We listened to 'em all night.' 'Like hell,' I said. 'Don't go walking in there.' So he circled to the right of this grassy knoll. He sent Sergeant Brown in there with his squad. We heard a couple of shots. 'Brown's in trouble,' he said. 'I'm going down there.' "

John Stankus told his brother that he would go along. The two went down into the valley behind the knoll. John heard a sound behind him, and spun to see a Japanese raising his rifle. John squeezed off two shots. The first hit the man in the chest, the second in the head—"The poor bastard had tangled up his rifle in the vines."

"Dig in," John told his brother. "We're going to be in for a bad time."

Four times in the next four hours pockets of Japanese rushed the Stankus brothers. Four times they turned back

135

the enemy. Then the rest of Henry's company showed up, and the lost battalion came down and hit the Japanese on the opposite side. When the F-2-5 took the offensive, Henry led a marine bayonet attack, but he got shot in the leg. The next casualty was J. B. Doyle, hit by a falling tree torn loose from the wet soil by the concussion of the Sherman guns.

Henry fashioned a splint for his leg out of a Japanese bayonet, and John hoisted him over his shoulder and carried him out.

John returned to the site. Sometime later, he was sitting in a clearing with his friend Kaltenbaugh. Kaltenbaugh was sitting on a bump in the ground. It started to move. He asked John if he thought the volcano was acting up. John told him to get up quickly, grab the grass on top of the bump and yank on it.

"It was a Jap spider hole," John Stankus told me. "He'd been sitting on them for hours!"

Stankus emptied fifteen rounds into the hole and killed the two men.

"We finished the whole thing in six hours," John Stankus told me. "That was the battle of Nameless Hill."

We drove to the airfield and hiked several hundred yards, fording a stream, to reach the wreckage of the American plane. We found its wing a few hundred feet in front of the fuselage; the plane had come in too low and rammed into a hillside.

Popsy's son Morris found two empty canteens in the fuselage of the wingless plane; his younger brother stood nearby and played with a seed pod which, if tossed into the air, circled slowly to the ground like a helicopter rotor.

Down the road, at another site behind a thatched cottage on stilts, we inspected a pile of discarded wings from various planes, strangely disembodied. An old woman from the cottage handed us several coconuts. A young boy with a machete chopped them open for us, and we drank, and ate the meat, passing the coconuts among us in silence. We stopped to look at a half-dozen amtracks, and while the boys looked on, I carefully inscribed in the rust on the back of one, with my forefinger, my father's initials and unit.

An hour after arriving in Gloucester I had already begun to feel the war more strongly than on Guadalcanal—not only because so much wreckage was strewn so matter-of-factly across the landscape here, exactly where it had been left, but also because here, in the absence of anything modern, I felt time slow down to Popsy's pace. I quickly learned that in Popsy's village, if something didn't get done in the morning, it would get done in the afternoon, and if not in the afternoon, the next day. If Charles said he'd be back in fifteen minutes, he might be back in five hours: time didn't matter because there was nothing more important at the end of it than what was happening now, in the middle of it.

On New Britain the plodding tempo of the jungle Pacific war seemed not only real to me but very close. In Guadalcanal, even the gruesome sorrow of the scene at Edson's Ridge had been punctuated by the whine of an Air Niugini 737's jet engine at the adjacent airfield. But here the wreckage was preserved as if in temporal aspic. While on Edson's Ridge I could imagine the echoes of the trumpets of battle as wave after wave of screaming Japanese charged my father's men, here, as I dug a bullet out of the mound in which it had sat for fifty years—undisturbed, in the middle of the jungle—something tilted off center for a minute, and I was oddly elated and frightened at the same time.

The mound of dirt that Popsy's kids had led us to was invisible to my untrained eye, which took it in as nothing but a natural feature of the thick jungle, so overgrown and clotted with foliage that I could see nothing other than the vines and the tree trunks. It lay about a hundred yards into the jungle off the road, a mound of dirt about ten feet wide and three feet high. I had hidden behind mounds just like it with my plastic tommy gun in Bronxville as a kid, except this one had been used for real. As they were chased away from the airfield, down the coast toward the Talasea Peninsula in the middle of the island, the Japanese had erected dirt walls behind which they could ambush the advancing marines. They were effective barriers, because the dirt was so soft that the American bazooka shells wouldn't detonate in them.

Apparently this one had been the site of a significant firefight: the village kids regularly came out to find bullets in it, and the supply was apparently inexhaustible because it took me just a few seconds of digging with a stick to find mine: perfectly round in the front, flat at the back, fired from a marine rifle.

"The boys shoot birds with the bullets," Charles told me. "They use catapults"—slingshots—"and they use the bullets to kill the birds."

I slipped the bullet into my pocket, and felt for it over the next several days. I would keep this one, I decided.

The kids went back to the car. I turned to walk the hundred yards back to the road. After about thirty seconds of walking, I realized I'd gone in the wrong direction. I turned around and could no longer see the bunker, or the clearing we'd been in. It was only when one of the boys returned to the spot to look for me, and I spied his red shirt through the trees, that I realized where I was. For a moment the jungle had swallowed me—on a sunny, clear day.

"My god, to try to see something, you know, was almost impossible," Richard Nellson told me. Nellson was a captain in the 1-5. "You'd get bogged down in the rain. Even these jeeps with four-wheel drive we thought were next to god—my lord, even *they* couldn't make it."

"You'd end up throwing a lot of grenades in the dark. In one instance we heard this business on the perimeter, and we heard this thrashing around down below, and we figured we were going to be in for it. We waited and waited —we waited so long my guys were going to kill me—and I said, 'Pull pins!' and 'Heave!' Down they went. And, my God, all we got out of there was, 'Oink! Oink! Oink! Oink!' "

Endless patrols through solid rain. The longest march for the 1-5, down the spine of the island south of Natamo in search of a fleeing Japanese admiral, was supposed to last half a day, and ended up lasting twenty-one days. It rained every day, and the men had no change of clothes. The bottom of Larry Sheridan's feet rotted right off and he ended up on crutches for a month waiting for another layer to grow back.

"Our rations were so low, two men were sharing one K ration a day," Russ Clay told me. "The airdrops couldn't find us because of the jungle. We were eating the shoots on the inside of coconut-tree sprouts. You'd pull 'em out and they tasted like asparagus. I must have eaten about a hundred pounds of them."

"There was more danger from the treetops crashing in the rainstorms than the Japanese artillery at that point," H. L. Opie remembered. His real name is Hierome. He was a machine-gun-company commander on Gloucester for the 1-5. What H.L. remembers is the jungle rot. The patrols went on forever, and led nowhere—until, from a few yards away, a shot rang out, or a shell fell, or a mortar took out the lead man.

In a way, Gloucester was the worst kind of war. It lacked the drama of open-field engagements and full-scale attacks. It was a war that sapped you.

"You know, I used to think people were yellow if they couldn't take it," Maurice Raphael told me. "But then we had a corpsman with us who'd been with us on Guadalcanal. And this youngster, he was patching people and doing great on Guadalcanal. Right in the thick of it. Then all of a sudden, on a patrol on Gloucester, a few rounds of mortar came in and this kid cracked wide open. He started screaming and hollering. We sent him to the back. And then I realized that people weren't yellow—it's just that everybody has a different breaking point. I reckon I had to withdraw my statement about yellow. People I used to think were yellow just had an earlier breaking point."

"A couple of snipers could hold up a whole battalion for a week," is what Leonard Lawton recalled of New Britain. "They could hide behind the roots of the Banyan trees.

"It was a stupid kind of war," Leonard Lawton says now, almost angrily.

Back at the compound, I told Popsy about the significance of the hill in whose shadow he lived. I told him that he was raising his family in the shadow of Target Hill.

He pointed to the top of the crest.

"There is a gun on top of the hill," he said. "A Japanese soldier fired the last shot from the gun, and then walked to Talasea."

I asked Popsy if he'd ever climbed up to see it. He laughed loudly and heartily. A foolish question.

Target Hill was called Sankokuyama by the Japanese, who had used it as an observation post prior to the invasion, until the preinvasion bombardment denuded it; it was relinquished with minor opposition at the start of the invasion.

But it was on Target Hill that the Japanese mounted their first organized counterattack, scaling its steep sides with several determined companies. At times the American mortars were raining scant yards in front of the American defenders, so steep was the slope.

"We got our butts kicked on Target Hill," one of my father's officers had told me, although the Japanese never regained the place. In fact, history says the Seventh Regiment took the brunt of it on Target Hill, which was notable primarily for the ferocity—and battle ignorance—of one Lieutenant Colonel Abe, whose conduct epitomized the Japanese style of jungle fighting: fierce, persistent, and not very smart. Abe led his troops right at the strength of the marines, who had been stretched thinly across the ridge. A more measured attack might have broken through the marine lines; instead, one of Abe's officers made the charge screaming at the top of his lungs, which served only to give the marine gunners a specific target in the dark. The marines poured gunfire into the jungle where he was yelling, and the yelling stopped, as did the charge.

Some 200 Japanese were killed in hand-to-hand combat on Target Hill. When Abe was found, he was wearing two pairs of pants, three shirts, and a raincoat. A heavy pack was on his back, and a coat strapped to the pack. He carried a sword, a pistol, an entrenching tool, and field glasses. All this to charge up a steep hill in the jungle in the rain. It was headstrong, valiant, and irrational.

They found a personal effect in Abe's pack: a receipt for a sweater purchased in Manila.

A good half-dozen village children joined me for the climb up Target Hill, along with a man named Tiggy, of an indeterminable age, a spritelike man whose smile never faded. I don't know where he had come from. He was just always there. A kid with a machete led the way. The boy directly in front of me pushed various branches out of the way. With one, he carefully pushed the leaves out of the way with a stick. "That vine bite you," he said.

I soon knew what he meant. The vines attacked me from behind, too. For the first time, I'd taken the jungle too lightly, and I'd worn shorts. Within a half hour, serrated and sawtoothed vines had laced the backs of my calves, drawing lines of blood in crisscrossed patterns above my knees and on the back of my calves.

The topography of the hill provided a lesson in jungle warfare. Craters depressed the jungle floor. Humps of earth rose where they shouldn't have been. I caught a glimpse of the odd piece of rusted metal, hidden back in a thick glade grown nearly dark.

The slope turned steep; I had to grab at the vines hanging down everywhere like ropes to propel myself up. On Guadalcanal I'd climbed the mountain with two men in their thirties. Here I was with a band of kids who skipped up the trail as if they were butterflies flitting across a meadow; their feet barely seemed to bother to touch the ground. I'd coyly stop as if to explain some finer point, but usually it was to catch my breath. My heart was beating so hard I figured it had to give out; the closest hospital was hundreds of miles away. So I stopped. The children understood. They waited, impassively, regarding me with curiosity.

Just beneath the crest, a machine-gun stand filled a large foxhole, pointing toward the crest. It was positioned to repel attacks. I climbed down into the pit. The children stood at the top of the ridge, looking down at me, and there I was, as if at the lecture podium in college, with the class spread up around me, and without even taking notice of what I was doing, I suddenly found myself telling them the tale of Target Hill, of the dramatic and brave and foolhardy charges by the Japanese infantry. I felt foolish as I heard myself adopt, reflexively, the lecturer's tone. But the unblinking gaze of the audience kept me going. I don't imagine they understood a great deal of what I said. I don't even know if they were vaguely curious about the history of their homeland. But I was also telling my father's story, to whomever would listen, as if to get it on the record.

At the very top of the mountain we stopped in a small clearing to look at a Japanese ammunition case. "My grandfather said an American soldier is buried here," Michael McKenzie said. Michael was a twelve-year-old with a curious mind and a cheerful demeanor.

The top of the mountain furnished a clear view of Natamo Point, the crook of the bay, and the Twin Fork River running north into the sea, the waves lapping at the black sand, the palms bending to the water. It looked like a travel poster. I tried to imagine the concussion of Japanese guns on the point shelling the lip of the Twin Fork, the marines pinned on the beach, the cacophony. It was impossible. The only sound was the wind in the jungle—a sound very different from the sound of a breeze through a deciduous forest back home. Rope vines with their huge heart-shaped leaves, palm fronds, and the thick banyan trunks were everywhere: the wind here was playing a completely foreign set of instruments, and its music cast a spell.

As I stood watching the Point, the children stayed around me, completely still, saying nothing, watching the same thing I was watching because I was watching it. Then one of the boys spoke, and Tiggy translated for me: "I have seen the bones of dead men on Natamo Point. I have seen the jaw and the teeth."

Inland from Natamo Point, I could see another hill several hundred yards east of us. The Japanese called it Aogori Ridge. After January 11, 1943, to the marines it was never known as anything but Walt's Ridge. On Aogori Ridge, Lew Walt, my father's friend and his commander on Guadalcanal, first made his name as a soldier.

Walt landed on New Britain as the commander of the 2-5, a lieutenant colonel. The next week they made him executive officer of the entire Fifth Regiment. It was Lew Walt who was responsible for the drive to the southeast, the pivot on which the entire campaign balanced. The Japanese had relinquished the airfield without much of a fight, but they were drawing the line in the hills just north of Borgen Bay to make their last stand. There were three hills standing between the marines and the Japanese regimental headquarters.

Walt was temporarily given command of the 3-5 and went after the Aogori Ridge. According to several histories, Walt's battalion spent the entire day of January 9 trying to take the hill, to no avail.

"To the Japanese," wrote Frank Hough in *The Island War*, "it was now or never, and they knew it. That ridge had been entrenched like nothing the Marines had yet encountered in all this long and savage drive. In addition, the steepness of the slope made the mere climbing a torture. Several times they got almost to the top, only to have to fall back before positions which could not be liquidated. Knowing that his exhausted men were close to the end of their ropes, Walt finally resorted to as odd a bit of tactical innovation as has ever been produced by a Corps famous for improvisation. He ordered a 37mm gun brought up, the largest weapon there was any possible chance of handling in such terrain. This was hauled as close as possible by an amphtrack, then manhandled to the most advanced position. There he loaded with canister and fired straight ahead, blasting Japs and jungle alike. Into the opening thus created, the gun was hauled forward and fired again. And so on. Weary men dragging, lifting, prying a half-ton of gun through a mangled jungle up a slope that seemed as steep as the side of a house."

A letter from then Brigadier General J. T. Selden to Hough elaborates: "Walt called for volunteers. There were none forthcoming. He then grabbed the 37 himself and attempted to push it up the ridge. In doing so, he pulled both arms out of their shoulder sockets. Walt [then] had plenty of volunteers."

"It was nearly dusk," Hough wrote, "when they made the top. Immediately they dug in, utilizing Japanese emplacements. Repeated new Japanese attacks roared up out

145

of the valley. It was not until daylight that the staring-eyed, slack-jawed survivors of 3/5 knew with any certainty that they had won.

"It is quite possible," Hough wrote, "that the real climax of the Cape Gloucester campaign occurred there that night."

One of my father's soldiers, a man named Ray Fenton, who lasted two days in my father's battalion on Peleliu before taking a two-inch piece of shrapnel in his neck, told me about the legendary friendship between my father and Lew Walt.

"Well," Fenton said, "you know that it was Walt and your father who wrestled that gun."

Which gun? I said.

"The 37-millimeter. On Gloucester."

I asked him if he was certain.

"Oh, sure," Fenton said. "The first time I met him, he was joking about how hard that had been."

The books only refer to Walt's Ridge. The Richmond name would have to find its own private place.

It was growing dark as we descended the other side of Target Hill. I stumbled down the trail, tripping over vines, doing my absolute best to keep from pitching headlong into the jungle: It seemed unlikely that we'd find our way off the mountain in the dark. But, of course, suddenly there was a trail, and then a dirt road, and we were walking back toward the village; it was nearly dark. We stopped by the side of the road to look at a large bunker of dirt.

"When the battle was over," Michael McKenzie, the twelve-year-old, told me, "the marines emptied their weapons here." Michael was explaining to me, in the dusk—

nearly completely dark now—that the birds they killed with their bullet slingshots are called flying foxes—"We break their necks"—when something extraordinary happened: as he was speaking, a very small star of light flashed from his mouth. I'd never seen anything like it, except in special-effect movie scenes. It even had points, the star—not five symmetrical points, but tiny lines, a burst of light in a microsecond.

A shudder flashed up my back; I first thought that it was simple exhaustion, except that there were no dots floating in front of my eyes, nor was I dizzy or faint. Only one explanation seemed possible: I was being signaled.

I was being told that I had come to the right place.

I was being told that whatever I had come for, I had found it.

I have no truck with mystical things. I believe in nothing but the things that I can see. But I saw the star flash out of Michael's mouth, and I know it was real. I also know that there's no room for fantasy in adulthood, and that the older we get, the less mystical the world must, by necessity, appear.

That night I sat on the steps of my house, sipping orange soda from the refrigerator that didn't keep anything cold, and watched Popsy and his friends drink Jack Daniels next to a trash can full of burning wood. They had a tape deck. It was playing the soundtrack of "Georgie Girl," as sung by Petula Clark. When the song ended, I heard a pounding sound, and at first I couldn't identify it. It seemed familiar, but I could make no sense of it.

It was the surf. The waves were pounding rhythmically onto the black sand. I walked down the steps, across the dirt road, and onto the black beach. The stars were plentiful, but it was the darkness of the sand on the beach that seemed so strange. It was as if there were nothing beneath my feet. As if I were floating.

The next morning I walked again to the beach where, on the black sand, a thousand tiny black sand crabs, half an inch long, were rolling the black sand into a thousand perfect tiny spheres that looked like very small ball bearings. I could not imagine what the crabs were going to do with them. They would be washed away by the tide. Then they'd do it all again later.

Down the bay I could see Natamo Point. I was waiting for Charles and his friend to take me down by boat. They'd offered to do so first thing this morning, but I wasn't holding my breath. I walked back to my house, and sat down in the garage space beneath the house, displacing a couple of roosters. Within a couple of minutes a woman and her daughter wandered over and smiled. I didn't speak pidgin and they didn't speak English, so I just handed them the book about the battle at New Britain.

Within a few minutes men, women, and children had appeared from nowhere, and a crowd of a dozen passed the book back and forth.

I leaned back and sipped an orange soda, and found I wasn't even bothering to shoo the flies away. After a while you hardly noticed them.

With Target Hill and Hill 660 and Walt's Ridge captured, the battle for New Britain was over, for all practical purposes. All that remained was for the marines to chase the Japanese east, back to Rabaul. In fact, the marines eventually let them go back to Rabaul and stay there, some 20,000 of them; thereafter, they were not a threat.

The Fifth Regiment had been entrusted with sweeping

the beach going due east in the region known as Borgen Bay, a stretch of beach that curled down in a half-circle to the river known as the Twin Fork, then back up again to Natamo Point. They found the going easy until, on the twentieth of January, a patrol from the Fifth Marines encountered fire from the Point, and found themselves stopped on the western bank of the Twin Fork.

A Japanese map, captured on January 3, had shown the presence of several machine guns and a couple of platoons on the Point. The marines had figured it would be an easy fight. It wasn't. Two days of artillery could not weaken the Japanese opposition, which now appeared to consist of automatic cannons and 75-mm field guns. Patrols were stopped at the river. It was later discovered that trails inland from Natamo Point led south to the Japanese regimental headquarters; hence the strong fortifications up the coast.

John Stankus, the regimental scout, first discovered the strength of the Japanese out on the point. The regimental response was to send a couple of companies of the 1-5 up the beach.

Larry Sheridan was a corporal in D-1-5. He remembers being pinned down by a shore gun on the western shore of the point. He was the first soldier to greet my father's arrival at the scene—unofficially, at any rate.

"We were under fire," Sheridan said, "and this little guy came up with this poncho and helmet on. He looked like a turtle with the helmet that was too big and the poncho that was too big.

" 'Corporal Sheridan?' he said, and he started asking questions. I said, 'I don't know who the hell you are, but get the hell out of here.' He said, 'I'm Major Richmond. I'm the new battalion exec.' And he laughed like hell. Todd

Buchmiller was riding my ass about it—'Jesus Christ! Leave it to you to chew out the executive.' But your father had a lot of common sense that a lot of leaders don't have. You could talk to him."

Pinned between the river and the bay, D company was facing some of the hardest concentrated Japanese fire of the campaign. Sheridan watched as bullets took out his first machine-gunner, and then, as soon as he'd moved up, his second. And then his third.

"They had a field piece out on the point firing at us across the bay," Sheridan said. "They had machine guns. They had a 37 in the road up ahead of us and they fired, and one of the guys said, 'Goddamn, that sun is hot.' I said, 'Hot my ass—that's the muzzle blast.' They'd just blown it right over us. We got the mortars to take them out.

"Then that little guy from New York showed up."

"We were getting pinned down, and along this trail we had been on comes a tank," Robert Amery told me. Amery was a gunnery sergeant with the A-1-5.

"This young fellow is directing the tank. He's walking in front of it. We were all laying on the ground, and the Japanese were firing all around us. We yelled, 'Hey, watch out! Get down! They're shooting down here!' But it didn't bother him a bit. Didn't bother him a bit, and he's still signaling the tank. After that, with the tank in there we were able to advance."

My father, carrying a horseshoe in his back pocket.

"I thought he was exposing himself quite a bit," Amery said. "Sometimes I thought he was on the reckless side. And he seemed so young to be a major. But you age fast."

"He was fearless," Leonard Lawton told me. Lawton was on the Point, too. "He never acted as if anyone was ever going to shoot at him. Was he ever decorated?" Leonard Lawton asked me.

I told him that my father had won a Silver Star on Natamo Point, and a Bronze Star for an action in a locale I hadn't been able to identify.

"I didn't know if he ever got them," Lawton said. "I know he deserved them."

"The point was like a forefinger sticking out into the bay, and we were on the thumb," Bill Looney recalled. Looney had the machine-gun company of the 1-5. He offered the opinion to one of his commanding officers that the machine gunners in the companies on the front were revealing their position and drawing Japanese fire by firing too-long bursts.

"We were trying to get out to the tip of the finger. Some of our troops were at the bottom knuckle of the finger, but I didn't like the way it was done. I suggested it was done wrong. I guess I made a jackass of myself. I told someone that the machine guns from my company were much better trained than the guns that belonged to the companies. They turned around and used mine the second day.

"The next day your dad was up there with C Company. Your dad was running the show."

My father was given a reinforced company to sail down the bay to land at the mouth of the Twin Fork, with some medium tanks and DUKW. The DUKW was new to the marines; it was an Army amphibious vehicle equipped with wheels instead of treads, and a honeycombed rocket launcher on its back. The rockets made a whooshing sound when they were fired—a deceptively unimpressive sort of exhalation; initially the marines laughed at the sound, but when they had an opportunity to see the damage the rockets did when they reached the end of their flights, they stopped laughing.

The reinforced company was dropped on the other side of the estuary, to help C Company, which was commanded by John McLaughlin. They were pinned in place by mortar and machine-gun fire. The Japanese were holding the point more steadfastly than anticipated. My father set up the company in a defensive posture and directed patrols into the jungle to scout the size of the Japanese position.

"Your father took over everything," Rocco Zullo told me. "Provided the artillery fire, the mortar fire, all the advancing to be done. Through all the fighting he was level-headed, cool-headed, always knew what he was doing."

Hank Paustian remembers going out on one of the patrols with my father when he first arrived; the patrol came so close to the Japanese that Paustian could hear them chopping down trees to improve their fortifications in the jungle. The patrol turned back. Paustian had no idea who the new man on patrol was.

"He was just wearing fatigues," Paustian told me. "I was bumming cigarettes off him—a real calm, cool, collected guy just walking with us. I found out later who he was. I was a little embarrassed after that."

Why?

"Because I'd bummed cigarettes off him and didn't call him 'sir.' "

• • •

I'd found out that he won his Silver Star on Natamo Point because I'd been able to procure a copy of his Silver Star citation, even though the Military Personnel Records division of the National Personnel Records Center hadn't answered my letters. His medals and awards records were not part of his service record, and I'd been instructed to write under separate cover to the awards division to find out specifically how he'd earned them. I was told it could take up to six months or a year to get an answer from the awards division, so I'd called up the Marine Corps Headquarters in Washington and told the corporal on the other end of the line that I didn't have the time to wait for a response from St. Louis—that I was going overseas, and wanted to know exactly what my father had done to win a Silver Star. He told me to hold on, and came back to the phone and said that he had a copy of the Silver Star citation. He'd be glad to fax it, he said, and he did so immediately.

"With a small patrol of volunteers," it read, "he advanced inland to pass around the enemy's left flank and, after hours of tedious maneuvering, led his patrol into the midst of hostile defenses to observe the positions of the Japanese as well as the number of personnel. Withdrawing by the same route, he initiated an aggressive attack on the following morning and destroyed the enemy, thereby securing the west side of Borgen Bay. By his leadership, courage and devotion to duty, Major Richmond contributed materially to the success of our operations against this heavily fortified Japanese stronghold and upheld the highest traditions of the United States Naval Service."

"I did not know it at the time," Bill Looney told me, "but I learned several days later that Tom had gone on a scouting trip by himself the night before and waded in a swampy river up to his chest to determine the strength of the Japanese force we would take on the next day. This was some kind of man."

Tom Panouses was a PFC in the C-1-5. He took part in the first attack after my father's reconnaissance patrol. He remembers approaching the point by wading in the same river my father had traversed the night before.

"Our whole doggone platoon, including a machine gun and a rifleman and a BAR, we were shoulder deep in water," Panouses told me. "We had to go in there quietly so that we didn't make any noise in the water. If you picked up your feet the wrong way, it'd make a sucking sound, you know? We got up to the point to where the ground started coming up. We set the tripod down. Set the machine gun down. One of the riflemen got spotted by a Jap who came out to urinate. He started to scream to let the other Japs know we were there. So we opened fire. We started spraying those goddamn guys coming over the ridge and knocking them down. I remember picking up that damn machine gun without my asbestos glove.

"We ran through two hundred fifty rounds. We started back out and ran through that damn water. Took us forever to get in there, but it took us fifteen minutes to get out. The next day they counted fifty-one dead Japs from that patrol."

When I asked Larry Sheridan about Natamo Point, it wasn't my father he remembered. It was about how that one battle, lost to history, insignificant to everyone but a handful of principals, epitomized his war and the marines. Larry Sheridan, like all of them, had not spoken of these things for decades, by choice. But now, given the chance, he chose to elaborate.

"We bitched a lot, but when the situation called for it, we were there. Natamo Point is a perfect example. When Cochran's squad got hit, Shereika took over. When Shereika got hit, someone else took over. Each one just automatically moved up into fire because you've been trained to do that.

"You know, we used to bitch like hell because we hated to do machine-gun drill: in the hot sun and the sand, you'd say, 'Sonofabitch! When are we going to stop this bullshit?' But when we first got a real good dose of it on Natamo Point, we just did it.

"It was a great cadre of people," Larry Sheridan told me.

Charles and Tiggy showed up about noon to take me across the bay to the point, in the boat with the outboard. We were delayed a hundred yards offshore when, for some reason, Tiggy misunderstood something Charles had said, and picked up the anchor and threw it out into the water. There was no rope attached to it. Charles laughed. I chalked it up to betel nut. Embarrassed, Tiggy dove to the bottom a few dozen times and found it, and we puttered across Borgen Bay, on water as deep as a dark night.

The small village on Natamo Point consisted of seven or eight huts on stilts, rising from the dirt, surrounding a large patch of bare dirt in the center of which sat a large rusted American bomb casing, alone, like a monument. Nearby, at the edge of the trees, hundreds of cans—soda cans, food tins—lay piled in a pit a few feet deep and ten yards wide. It was once a bomb crater, now a garbage pit.

Charles sat on the bomb while Tiggy explained our mission to some of the men who had come out of their huts to see about the white man who had shown up on their peninsula in the middle of the day.

Only one of the villagers had lived through the war. He was in his sixties, and he was wearing a skirt and holding a large stick. His earlobes were long, hanging a few inches, and each earlobe had a large hole in it.

He spoke to me. I asked Tiggy what he had said.

"He said, 'I was afraid of the guns and the bombs.' "

Charles stayed behind with the villagers to chew betel nut. Charles thought I was out of my mind. Walking into the jungle was not what Charles intended to do on a very hot day. He intended to do nothing but chew betel nut, the way the crabs chose to roll the black sand into little spheres that would be erased by the waves. The high that lacquered Charles and Popsy and the rest of their friends, I eventually decided, was their way of tempering the realities of a hostile nature: volcanoes, tsunamis, infant mortality. Charles and the crabs had signed a more realistic pact than I had in life: short life, nothing accomplished, but the occasional feast of pig and freshwater eel.

We were walking up a dusty road when I happened to glance to the side of the trail, into the bush, and I saw a finger of muddy water snaking beneath drooping vines. I knew immediately that it was the river my father had waded in. It was nearly stagnant, and black mud lined its shores. Insects dotted its surface, the water a curious cross between café au lait and pea soup. I would no sooner have waded in the creek than I would have swallowed bleach. In the middle of the night he would not have been bothered by its color.

• • •

According to the Marine Corps monograph, the 1-5 spent the next two days "in a series of short sharp skirmishes" securing the next five hundred yards of coastline, heading eastward, on the road we were presently walking on: Tiggy; a Natamo villager, an older man named Joe Kamu; and Michael McKenzie. Michael's English was excellent.

"Mr. Peter? The president of America is George Bush?"

No, I explained. It's Bill Clinton.

"What happened to George Bush?"

I explained the electoral process.

"Mr. Peter?" said Michael. "How many states are there in America? Do you have coconuts in your country? Do you have brothers and sisters?"

He was asking questions simply for the sake of asking questions. To tap my brain for whatever it was he could get from it.

"Mr. Peter," said Tiggy. "Chuck Berry is American?"

Yes, I told him.

"Michael Jordan is American?"

Yes, I told him.

"He's giant, no?"

Yes, I said. He's a giant.

We followed the creek as it wound in and out of the jungle, and then lost it. Now we were following a parched dirt road. To the side of the road an area about a hundred yards square had been fenced off with reed walls. Tiggy explained that the village held its weekly dances here. It was in the same area that the skirmishes had been held.

"Rock and roll," Tiggy said, and the boys giggled.

The dance floor was dirt, except where the rusted universal joint of an overturned truck, buried for fifty years, poked through the surface.

We walked farther up the road, and farther still, until I realized that Tiggy and Michael and Joe were following me, and I wasn't going anywhere in particular—just down the road, away from the shore. I knew from reading various accounts that a 1-5 combat patrol had had some firefights along this trail. My friends didn't find it strange, I guess, that we weren't going anywhere; they had nothing to do. So we walked up the road a couple of miles—the route that the fleeing Japanese would have taken, heading east, after my father had routed them off the point. Michael and Tiggy and Joe showed not the slightest sign of fatigue. I was trying to be cool, but eventually I felt I was going to melt into a puddle. Tiggy, sensing my foolishly stalwart demeanor, suggested we duck into the undergrowth to rest; I sank into the coolness of the jungle as if I were falling underwater.

Michael tore a few dozen palm leaves off some bushes, wove them into a rope, strapped one end of the rope to each of his ankles, and shimmied up a palm tree in two seconds flat. A moment later, coconuts were raining down from the sky. I drank one in a single gulp, slashed the top off another, and sat on the jungle floor.

"My father was a boy in Milne Bay when the Japanese came," Michael told us. "He took his sister and went into the bush."

Joe Kamu told us that his own father had fought with the Japanese.

As soon as my eyes adjusted to the gloom beneath the jungle canopy, I saw a rusted gas tank riddled with bullet holes, mounted to what was left of a small chassis. It must have been a jeep. It was on the road up which the 1-5 had chased the Japanese.

Back in the village Charles was still sitting on the bomb, doing betel nut, dipping his stick into the lime and licking it. At the sight of our approach he grinned. I told him he could take his boat back across the bay without me; I was going to walk down the beach toward Gloucester, retracing the 1-5's advance. It was a walk of only three kilometers, but to Charles it was sheer lunacy. He kept asking me if I was certain. I was certain. Tiggy and I set out down the trail just inland from the beach, and when I turned around, there were four more kids with us, from the Natamo village.

"They say there is a large gun down the trail," Tiggy said. It turned out the gun wasn't there, but the emplacement was: a heavy cylindrical mount, with four legs rotting into the jungle floor. It would have been aimed down the beach at the marines. It would have been the gun that had the marines pinned down at the Twin Fork River.

"Papa b'long em ibin kam long Cape Gloucester," Tiggy was telling the kids. *"Nait long twelve midnait em igo long Natamo Point we camp b'long Japaness na em bihain wanpela wara ikam isi isi ikam daun long wara na i lukum ol Japaness pinis bihain igo bek long U.S.A. camp nam igo na tokim olgeta soldier na ol ikam bek long nait around twelve midnait nal ol pait igo kam na kilim olgeta Japaness bihain war pinis na igo bek long America."*

Which I took to mean, more or less, that my father came down the point, scouted the Japanese, went back, got his soldiers, came back and killed all the Japanese. I couldn't keep up with the rest of the pidgin, but as I watched the kids listen to Tiggy's story, I knew that history was being recorded. That if the history books were short on mentions of Tom Richmond, I'd done my part—at least at Cape Gloucester—to rectify the situation.

In fact, with any luck, by now Tiggy is telling the story of how General Tom Richmond had wiped out an elite battalion and turned the tide of the war. On Richmond Point.

After the battle on Natamo Point, the Puller patrol followed the trails inland, and finally discovered the headquarters of the Japanese commander. It was deserted. The marines returned to the coast, satisfied that they had cleared West New Britain of the enemy, and boarded small boats to hop down the coast, toward Talasea, trying to track the Japanese flight. Occasionally the boats would be fired upon. Occasionally the marines would land and spend the night and engage in firefights. The landing at Talasea was largely uneventful; scattered skirmishes marked the several days of the occupation before the division was called back east, its work on New Britain done.

"Talasea was a beautiful place," Robert Shedd told me. "High above the bay I remember looking out one day at a great big canoe full of the native boys with their paddles. What a picture.

"We used to do an awful lot of patrolling. I remember my squad leader always seemed to be sick when it was time to patrol. We used to go down towards the base of the peninsula and spend the night and come back . . . we never ran into much. One day this poor old Japanese man came up and I thought we'd capture him, and one of the guys got excited and killed him.

"He was a defenseless guy," Shedd said. "He couldn't have hurt anybody."

On the walk back from Natamo, I veered into the jungle toward the stream, looking for random wreckage, and the kids didn't think anything odd of it; they'd just follow me until the bush was too thick to navigate. Then I'd go on by myself, ducking beneath branches, tugging at vines. It was not Tarzan's jungle; it was thick and fecund and impenetrable. One time when I turned back, I found myself face to face with a large pig. We looked at each other. He didn't have tusks. But he didn't seem happy.

He blinked. I walked on.

We reached the Twin Fork River. The kids swam and frolicked in the chest-high water, splashing each other. I floated for several minutes in the buoyant salty currents, and then we all walked back to the village.

I was to leave the next day.

The boys wanted to show me a last artifact—a huge shore gun, mounted in front of someone's house; the family were sitting on their porch, watching the night sky, drinking something and chatting in murmurs, quite accustomed to passing an evening in the company of a very large piece of artillery.

Then I said goodbye to the group at large. Michael McKenzie came forward and asked to shake my hand. We stood there, looking at each other. I don't know if he understood how hard I shook his hand.

I looked at their faces, the young and the old, and they looked back at me—the white man who had dropped out of the sky, unannounced, the only white man to ever show up in their village as neither a missionary nor an Australian aid worker, carrying history books full of pictures of Americans and Japanese killing each other over pieces of their land. And for all of the death, absolutely nothing had changed in Cape Gloucester.

I figured that if they wanted a lesson, or a moral, or a summation, all I could tell them was that men had died. For better, for worse, for no reason at all. But they had died, and deserved to be remembered.

I think they already knew.

At eight the next morning, knowing it could take a good five hours to mobilize the transportation, I reminded Popsy of my plane out, due at one that afternoon. He said he'd go find someone who had a radio to find out if the plane would be coming in as scheduled, and then he disappeared for several hours.

I passed the time with the women and children from the village, who gathered again on the concrete porch beneath my house, leafing through my books about New Britain. Tiggy came by, and gave me his billy as a souvenir. Charles showed up to reassure me, in his heavy-lidded fashion, that we'd make the plane. He saw my Walkman. I showed it to him, and when he slipped the earphones over his head, and the music of Joe Jackson filled his head, he started to nod so naturally that I immediately knew that the Walkman would be my gift to Charles, with Joe Jackson's album *Laughter and Lust.*

For the rest of the morning Charles did not take the earphones off. He sat beneath the house chewing betel nut

and listening to Joe Jackson. I wondered what he made of
the lyrics. In one song, in which Joe Jackson is bemoaning
the plethora of choices in a world marked by a dearth of
quality, Jackson sings, "What shall we do this evening?
Send out for some sushi and champagne?"

It's a good album. The first song on the first side is
called "It's Obvious." Joe Jackson, an unapologetic liberal,
includes this refrain: "So we starve all the teachers, and
recruit more Marines / How come we don't even know
what that means?"

By and large, through all the pendulum swings since Vietnam, the marines have managed to remain above the fray;
the word "marine" carries a heft all of its own, no matter
what the arena, whether it's the front page of the *New
York Times,* which invariably identified the troops in So-
malia not as soldiers but as marines, to the movies, where
even today filmmakers know how to milk the pride we feel
in the Corps. The producers of *Aliens* knew what they
were doing when they gave Sigourney Weaver a company
of marines to help her fight the monsters; they fought hard
and bravely, and the bravest among them, a woman, blew
up a grenade in the face of one of the monsters at the cost
of her own life. Jack Nicholson won an Oscar for his
portrayal of a marine general in *A Few Good Men.* He
was meant to portray a villain—a martinet of the worst
order—but his courtroom testimony, pleading the case for
the marine way of doing things—of defending freedom at
home—stole the film.

Not long ago I came across one of my grandmother's
poems, dated March 20, 1946, entitled "Tom Richmond,"

and obviously meant to be spoken to the cadences of "The Halls of Montezuma":

> *From the sandy shores of Cuba*
> *To the halls of Quantico*
> *To the far Pacific Islands*
> *Where the coconut palms grow*
> *You have played your "sweet potato"*
> *Through the most unlikely scenes*
> *While you went about the business*
> *Of United States Marines.*

Popsy returned, and said the plane would be on time, and I asked him if he didn't think we should go. He conceded that we probably should. As we pulled out of the village, I found myself waving at all the faces I'd come to recognize. We made a final stop at the grocery store; Popsy and Charles went inside, and came out with sodas, and handed one to me. Then we were on the road to the airfield, stopping only to pick up a half-dozen people on the way.

"You should stay one more day, Peter," Charles told me. "We would fish over there," and he pointed to an island that lay off the coast. It was the island you see on the cover of a travel magazine: white sand, blue water, pines waving. I knew that if I missed my flight, the rest of the precariously arranged trip would come tumbling down; I'd miss the flight from Hoskins back to Port Moresby, and thus the Port Moresby-to-Manila, and Manila to Koror, and Koror to Peleliu.

But I found myself thinking that if we were to miss the flight, I could always visit Palau another time.

We made it on time. The plane, of course, was late. We

waited under a giant banyan tree a hundred yards away from the airstrip, along with a couple dozen villagers who were there for no particular reason other than that it was a good place to be. A three-walled wooden lean-to stood empty nearby; in the rains, I supposed, it served as a shelter for passengers to wait for the plane.

Then I noticed a pickup truck several dozen yards away. It sat facing away from us, with its back to the natives under the tree.

"Malaysian loggers," Tiggy told me.

One of the Malaysians got out of the pickup, walked over to the shelter, and, in full view of all the villagers, unzipped his pants and relieved himself. Then he zipped his pants back up, walked back and got into the cab of the pickup. They were awaiting a coworker, due in on the plane.

Charles sipped at a beer. I could hear Joe Jackson in his earphones: "How come we don't even know what that means?" Well, Joe Jackson didn't know, but everyone else seemed to.

The plane came in. It was my pilot again. He greeted me, asked how it had gone. A few passengers had disembarked; one was a Malaysian man, whose hand was pumped by the men who had been waiting in the pickup. The three of them moved in a way that to me, after just four days, seemed spasmodic and hurried, as if I were watching them in time-lapse photography. They were full of the hurry. No one else here was. Not even the pilot, who was deliberate.

"Fix the alternator?" I said.

"Not yet," he said.

I sat in the copilot's seat.

He tried to start the left engine. It wouldn't start. So he started the right engine. It started. Then he tried the left engine again. This time it started, after gasping and coughing.

As we started to taxi, I looked over my shoulder, and my friends were waving and smiling: Tiggy and Charles and Popsy. I knew that Tiggy and Charles would be going back to get the boat to go fishing on the island.

As we pulled into the air, I told the pilot about Target Hill, and the gun emplacement. "Want to go down?" he said, and banked the plane onto its side, and suddenly we were a few hundred yards directly above Target Hill, circling. From above, it looked benign and beautiful.

He came out of the roll, and pointed the Cessna toward Hoskins. The thrum of the vibration began to lull me to sleep.

PART III
Peleliu

I WAS LOOKING for microfilm records of the muster rolls of the 1-5 in the records department of the Marine Corps Historical Center when a clerk told me that there might be a file on my father in the bank of gray metal filing cabinets that stood behind him. It had not occurred to me that a half-century later there would be a file anywhere on my father, but there was. It was a very small file. It held a yellowed newspaper clipping and a large glossy photograph.

The news story had appeared on the front page of a Yonkers paper. The headline read, YONKERS MAN A HERO IN ATTACK ON TULAGI. Quoting from a marine release, the story said my father's company had faced "withering machine-gun fire from pillboxes and dugouts." With this news, the report noted, my father's parents learned of their son's whereabouts for the first time since he had sailed from New River, North Carolina.

169

The photograph in the file depicted my father staring off at some tropical horizon, Hollywood-like, his hands on his hips, with some palm trees in the background. It was clearly the product of the marine public-relations machine. On the back of the photograph was this caption: "MARINE BATTALION COMMANDER—A veteran of Guadalcanal and New Britain campaigns is Major Harold T. A. Richmond, 28, of Dunwoodie Street, Yonkers, N.Y., youngest battalion commander in his famed Marine Division."

I knew nothing of my father ever having commanded a battalion. Commanding a battalion represented a quantum leap from second in command: As battalion exec, the second in command, a marine straddled the line between command post and battlefield. The battalion exec was the commander's link to his thousand men. The commander himself was in another league—in the First Division cabinet, as it were.

It turned out that my father was the commander of the First Battalion, Fifth Marines, for a couple of months on an island called Pavuvu in the Russell Islands, where the First Division trained after the New Britain campaign as it readied for its next assault. Major Barba had been sent home after New Britain, and until a new colonel arrived, the battalion was given to my father.

"When he became the battalion commander," Bill Looney told me, "he became somewhat distant. We lost him for a while. He wasn't our buddy anymore. He realized what his job was at that point, and he didn't mess with it."

The Russell Islands, a few hundred miles southeast of the Solomons, were a horrible place for a battle-frayed division to encamp. The Russells had been chosen with a disturbing lack of foresight: a general had flown over the islands and thought they looked nice enough from the air. It turned out that 90 percent of Pavuvu was impassable swamp. The three-month stay on Pavuvu was to become as legendary as the ten-month bacchanalia in Australia, but for nearly opposite reasons. On Pavuvu the conditions were raw enough to prompt more than one marine to surmise that their commanders knew exactly what they were doing: getting the troops angry enough to assault the crack troops they'd face in a few months on Peleliu.

In Australia my father and his friends had clearly enjoyed their share of female company. But, as the precocious battalion commander on the Russell Islands, my father's closest comrades were land crabs and rats. And rotting coconuts.

An abandoned coconut plantation stood on the only part of the island that wasn't swampland. One of the earliest Pavuvu casualties was a marine who incurred a fractured skull at the nightly outdoor movies. Thereafter, the marines were instructed to wear helmets to the movies.

The land crabs provided some measure of distraction; it was all the sport to go on jeep cruises whose sole object was to crush the crabs flat. They were so plentiful that when they'd crawl beneath the wooden planks surrounding the officers' tents, the collective orchestra of their clicking pincers kept the men awake at night.

"They were knee-deep," Ray Fenton told me. "Your dad and I were out every night. About once a week we would lift up all the planks and get out our shovels and beat the hell out of the land crabs for about three hours so we could sleep."

Adding to my father's dismay, I imagine, was the paucity of reptiles. None of the men could remember any snakes on Pavuvu, just rats. Hundreds of rats. Pavuvu was an island sprung from the imagination of a Melanesian Edgar Allan Poe.

"The rats crawled over your naked body," Jake Omdahl said. "They had these ice-cold feet. Everything about these huge rats was hot, but their feet were like ice."

The morale on Pavuvu was terrible—the lowest of the Pacific war. New Britain had been a nightmare; the First Division had arrived on Pavuvu with jungle rot on their feet and memories of feeding on plants plucked from the trail sides during their endless and confused pursuits of the fleeing Japanese. Anticipating something along the lines of the Aussies' steak-and-eggs hospitality, they were none too pleased at being forced to rest on an island as mealy and sodden as New Britain had been.

"We had a work party that was assigned to pick up rotten coconuts one night over at the officer's camp," Hank Paustian told me. "And morale was pretty low at that time. Instead of tossing them, we were slamming them into the truck, you know? We were making as much noise as we could. We were getting some growling out of the officers' tents, but it didn't do any good—we continued to bang the coconuts.

"A little while later Major Richmond came out. He said, 'You men are going to have to keep it quiet. I know you're tired, I know how you feel. But you gotta keep it down.'

"See, he could have come out and chewed us out and ordered it. But he did it gentlemanly. I never forgot that. That's one thing I remember about your father that said a lot about the way he was."

• • •

His diplomacy averted another incipient disaster a few days later. This test was more severe: the battalion decided to pull a hunger strike.

"They were just feeding us warmed-over C rations," Russ Clay told me. "The food was terrible. It was pathetic. The coffee was green sometimes. Sometimes it was yellow. It was pretty funky stuff."

Clay decided he'd had enough on the day he watched the cook fashion a raisin pie. For some reason the cooks always had enough raisins. "Only we had these coconut flies," Clay recalls. "They were like houseflies, only where a housefly leaves you alone when you shoo it, these things stuck to you. They just stuck to your arms. Well, I saw the cook make a raisin pie, only he was wiping these flies off his arms and into the pie."

Various company malcontents banded together and announced that they would eat no more. For three days whatever the cooks concocted had to be thrown out. Finally my father showed up. He listened to the complaints. He dismissed the organizers without losing his temper. He told George Hadzidakis—his enlisted pal from the mill towns of Massachusetts—to stay, and invited the sergeant into his tent.

"You, too, Hadzidakis?" my father said. Hadzidakis shrugged. "Why didn't you tell me?" my father asked.

"I figured you'd hear about it sooner or later," Hadzidakis said. "Besides, I didn't want to be a fink."

My father asked him what he could do. "Get better food," George said. Two days later the food was much better. Hadzidakis doesn't know what exactly my father did; all he knows, he says, is that my father didn't discipline anyone. He just got better food for the men.

Bob Amery remembers my father on Pavuvu. Remembers how surprised he was that a battalion commander would come to the aid of a staff sergeant who hadn't even shown up until New Britain—joining an outfit where, unless you had been on "the Canal," you weren't worth your weight in C rations.

Pavuvu represented the two-year point for a lot of men, and they were being rotated home. Robert Amery was a staff sergeant on Pavuvu in the A-1-5, and he was looking for a promotion. Amery took a written exam and a field exam and he was promoted to platoon sergeant, but in the meantime, an opening for a gunnery sergeant came up, a position generally held by far more experienced men, often much older; the gunnery sergeant more or less runs the company. The captain tells his lieutenants what to do, the lieutenants tell the gunnery sergeant, and the gunnery sergeant is the one who invariably goes out and does it.

Amery was given the duty on Pavuvu of running the firing range for the battalion rifle tests—no small responsibility. The entire battalion had to be tested and graded on the range in a short period of time.

"Well, while this was going on, Major Richmond was watching this, and he thought I was doing great," Amery told me. "And so did I. Now one day they brought out a tent to put all the ammunition and supplies in. We were all trying to put this tent up, and it was falling, and the next thing I know I'm on the ground knocked out. The ridge pole had come off and hit me on the head. All it did was make my head bleed. They took me to the hospital and bandaged me up.

"Next thing I know Major Richmond came to see me. Richmond said, 'Are you all right? Can you continue?' I thought I shouldn't, but I said, 'I'm okay.' I also happened to mention to him that I was studying for the gunnery sergeant's exam at the same time. Richmond says, 'Don't worry about it. As long as you keep firing the battalion, don't worry about your score on the gunnery sergeant's exam.' Well, we finished all the firing, and Richmond was very happy with this. And when the score come out for the gunnery sergeant's list, I was on it! I went in as a twenty-two-year old gunnery sergeant! There were two hundred twelve enlisted men in the company. I was the second senior officer."

Six weeks after the division's arrival in the Russell Islands, Lieutenant Colonel Robert Boyd arrived to take command of the 1-5. My father was relieved of his assignment. By all accounts, he was a little relieved to be reassigned.

"The day the new colonel was assigned as battalion commander," Bill Looney told me, "I remember Tom walking in and saying, 'I've just been relieved. I'm exec again. Where's the beer? I know you fellows have the beer.' "

Beer wasn't the only advantage to losing the battalion. When my father got back to his men, he could play volleyball again.

"We used to call him the Green Hornet," Looney told me, "because he always wore green GI underwear shorts when we'd play volleyball on Pavuvu. So we called him the Green Hornet. Not to his face, of course. You don't call a major 'Green Hornet' to his face."

Several months after I'd talked to Looney, a photograph

of the Pavuvu volleyball crew arrived in the mail: fourteen of them, posing for the camera, many of them in boxers. But not my father. He's wearing fatigue pants.

"He played volleyball like mad," Ray Fenton told me. "He wasn't spiking many, but he was a fighter. At his size he looked like he should have been back in grade school. He was well muscled. Then, most of them had to be muscled and quick, or they were dead. They were relatively [small men] in size because they didn't get shot so often. The Fleet Marine Force did not have people who were six-foot-seven."

Fenton paused, and he laughed.

"Then, by Peleliu, most of the kids in my platoon—I didn't want to ask when they were born. This was a war where people were very enthused, and I had a lot of young kids who were fourteen or fifteen years old. Some of the recruiters looked the other way. I had a runner who saved my life a couple of times. He was about fifteen. We called him Chuck. He'd never shaved."

Two years into the fight, Gordon Gayle told me, it wasn't only recruiters who looked the other way when someone wanted to join.

"We had people who went over the hill from their units to stow aboard to go to Peleliu," Gayle recalled. "So we said, 'All right—welcome aboard. If you're still alive when it's over, we'll make sure you don't suffer for it.' "

Most of them had no way of knowing that the famed First Marine Division luck was about to run out.

In 1981, I was working for the *San Diego Union*, a conservative and fairly penurious daily paper. One day the maga-

zine *Sports Illustrated* published a story about cocaine use
in the National Football League, and the author implicated
Chuck Muncie, one of the San Diego Charger stars. The
next day I looked up from my desk to see an assistant
sports editor coming out of the sports editor's office. The
editor looked at me and made the motion of an airplane
taking off with his right hand. I was to fly that afternoon
to New Orleans, Muncie's home. It was a rare assignment;
the *Union* was a sleepy paper in a sleepy town, and we
seldom spent money to chase stories.

There was only one daily flight to and from San Diego
to New Orleans, on Pan Am, via Las Vegas. I got a flight
to New Orleans that day, a Wednesday. I held an open
ticket for the one daily flight back.

The plane stopped in Las Vegas long enough for me to
play the slots for a few minutes, then took off for New
Orleans. I arrived in Kenner, the New Orleans suburb
where the airport is located, on Wednesday night, and
drove to an address that our football writer had dug up
for Muncie, in Kenner.

I rang the doorbell. The man who answered the door
told me that yes, Muncie had lived there once, but not for
a few years, and he had no idea where he lived.

The next morning I went to the tax assessor's office
in Kenner and looked through the records until I found
Muncie's name. I found the home in a wealthy new development, but there was no answer to the doorbell. I rang a
neighbor's doorbell. The neighbor told me that Muncie
and his wife had left a few days earlier to go on a vacation
to the Bahamas, and he had no idea when Muncie would
return.

I called my editor and told him what I'd found. I asked
him whether I should come back to San Diego the follow-

ing day, or stay in New Orleans and poke around. I fully
expected him to summon me home. But he wasn't a native
San Diegan. He'd recently arrived from the *Philadelphia
Bulletin,* and he believed in reporting. We debated both
sides. I told him I had no idea when Muncie would return,
and I'd be spending the company's dollars spinning my
wheels; on the other hand, I said, I could probably find
some old teammates, do some background work.

After several seconds of deliberation, my editor said,
"As long as we have you down there, why don't you stick
around a couple of days and see what you can come up
with? Then if he still doesn't show, we'll bring you home."

The next morning I went to Muncie's house; still no sign
of anyone. I spent the afternoon in the public library going
through microfilm of the *New Orleans Times-Picayune.* I
was vaguely aware, in the early afternoon, of rain and
thunder beating the sides of the library, but when I
emerged, about 4 P.M., the sun was shining and the pools
of rainwater were already evaporating on the side streets
of the French Quarter. I was walking through the Quarter
when I saw a line of people on the sidewalk. I had stumbled upon K-Paul's Louisiana Kitchen, Paul Prudhomme's
restaurant; at four-thirty people were lining up to wait for
the doors to open at five. I sat down at a large table next
to several people I didn't know. I fell into comfortable
conversation with the man to my left as I sipped a Dos
Equis beer. My crayfish étouffée arrived. I told the man I
was from San Diego.

"Lucky you weren't on that plane," he said. When I
asked which plane, he told me that a jet had crashed at the
airport that afternoon in a rainstorm. A jet en route to San
Diego. A 727. It had been climbing at three hundred feet
when wind shear slapped it down to a hundred feet. As the

pilot tried to climb again, his left wingtip clipped a tree and the jet turned onto its side, hit the ground, and did a cartwheel through a residential neighborhood. No one survived.

It was Pan Am 759. I had an open ticket on Pan Am 759. If my editor had told me the night before to come home, I would have been on it. Instead I spent five days covering it, until the last bodies had been identified in the converted Delta hangar, and traffic in Kenner had been halted for the final time as they trucked the pieces of the jet out of town, toward the warehouse in Washington.

When I came back to San Diego, I went to the newspaper library to look at how the paper had played my coverage of the crash. On the day after the crash, the paper had run a photograph of the arrivals board in the Las Vegas airport. Next to PAN AM 759, instead of ON TIME or DE-LAYED, was the legend SEE AGENT.

Fourteen years later a throng is crowding what appears to be a long bulletin board in the lobby of the Riviera Hotel in Las Vegas in the early afternoon of a 120-degree summer day. Apologizing, I have to shoulder my way through a half-dozen elderly gentlemen to see what they're looking at. Finally I muscle my way through, to face a sea of names: a thousand tags stuck to a board some twenty feet wide.

Each name belongs to a marine who served with the First Marine Division. Each displays a name, a unit, and a war. I am scanning the names when an elderly man wrapped in a cocoon of tobacco scent walks slowly to the board and sticks his tag onto its surface. The sticker reads JACK PARRISH. G-2-5. WWII.

Were you on Guadalcanal? I ask him. He regards me with a bit of curiosity. I do not look like a marine veteran. I do not look as if I belong here.

"I sure was."

Were you in the G-2-5 on the Canal?

"I sure was," he says.

"Then you must have known my father," I say. "He was your company commander."

The man's gaze focuses. Examines my face. Then his face blossoms, all suspicion sloughs away. "You're Tom Richmond's son?"

I nod. Jack Parrish thinks for just a moment, and then he says to me, "There wasn't a man in our company who wouldn't have followed him anywhere. He was a fantastic marine. I've never seen any better. I was like all the rest of them in our company. I would have followed him to my grave if I had to."

And he puts his right arm around my shoulders, and slowly, befitting the pace of an elderly man who has all the time in the world, leads me through the pack of soldiers into the ballroom that has been converted into a hospitality suite for the First Marine Division reunion, where a thousand marines fill a hundred tables, nursing a thousand cold beers and scotches and vodkas, visiting a past that still, fifty years later, defines, and illumines, and haunts their present.

For an assemblage of the most distinguished fighting force in the history of American warfare, they are an unremarkable lot now. It is the softness that comes with age, the calm that half a century of perspective bestows on a man who goes into adulthood asking not a great deal out of life, satisfied with having been allowed to leave the war with his life intact, and, perhaps, that of a good friend or two.

It comes also, of course, from a half-century of grieving for the ones still lost, and feeling the shame at having survived—at having not, at some point, done something more, having not acted a little more selflessly or a little more aggressively so that someone else might have been spared. Only one time when I was writing this story did a marine ask to go off the record. When he did, he said to me, "I'm a guilty survivor."

Their expressions are not the chiseled demeanors I expected, the Rushmore-stiff profiles I've seen in some of the modern marines with whom I've had occasion to talk. There's no strut here; smiles flit around their weathered faces. These men are, by and large, indistinguishable from any group of men in their seventies. You would not know them to be marines if you entered this ballroom by chance; you'd think them to be retired shoe salesmen or teachers or truck drivers.

This owes something to the physical slack: the seventy-eight-year-old body has not recently hiked for twenty miles with a sixty-pound pack on its back. But there's something more to it. The marine vets of the Second World War are quiet, in all ways. The Vietnam vets at the annual First Marine Division Association reunion have arrived with toy models of assault rifles to place in the middle of the table; their olive caps and sloganed T-shirts are predictable, and give them a hard edge. When someone whoops at a table in the middle of the sea of tables on the first afternoon of the reunion, it is a veteran of Korea; the man dancing on one of the chairs is not young, but spry. It is not that a World War II marine could not dance on a chair; it's that he wouldn't.

They drink from morning on into the day—the bartender in the ill-fitting cummerbund and linoleum smile is doing good business all day, every day—but there isn't a single eruption, not a single laugh too loud, a single argument, a single spasm of impropriety from the tables of marines who have been doing this for half a century now.

Some started drinking the day they came home, and haven't stopped, and for all of the obvious reasons. The silences at the tables come in lumps. It is not surprising that few of the stories are about the fighting.

"The ship we were on, the head was stopped up," Jack Parrish tells me. His friend Theron Cordray is at his side. They are drinking clear liquid from plastic cups. "The water wouldn't flow down. The place was a mess. Men were getting sick. Richmond asked the gunnery sergeant to get a detail together to go in there and unplug it. The gunny came back and said they couldn't do it. The guys were getting sick, and they couldn't go in there. So you know who came down and unplugged it himself? Richmond, that's who."

Theron Cordray nods in remembrance and stares at nothing in particular. I asked Jack if he can remember anything else about my father. He shakes a Pall Mall into his hand, lights it, and takes a pull of its smoke the way you or I might breathe.

"On Guadalcanal one time," Jack Parrish tells me, "your father said, 'As soon as the marines are off this island, I'm going to get every man here drunk.' And he was good to his word. As soon as we got to Australia, he ordered six barrels of beer for that company. There was not a sober marine there that night. Including your dad. He got up on a table and danced a little jig."

They crowded every table—veterans of the First Marines and the Fifth Marines and the Seventh Marines and the Eleventh Marines. There were few of them in the casinos. A white-suited representative of the city had opened the convention with a sallow imprecation—"Spend a lot of money!"—but he had misjudged his conventioneers; in Vegas, a city that preys unabashedly on the weak and the temptable, the marines provided the wrong target. They were largely oblivious to the craps tables and the slot machines. The turnout from their outfits at the annual convention dwindles down each year, to a number you can count on two hands, or one; spending the days in the cave of a casino doesn't cross their minds.

I'd expected to find them delighting in the retelling of the gory deaths of the Japanese, and the heroic exploits of their pals. Instead I find immediately, within two hours of planting myself in the middle of the sea of tables, that they've come for something entirely different: to see the only friends they'd ever had who understood the prime force that had shaped their lives—fighting the war for three years and living with it for fifty.

No one else had the slightest idea of what it had been like to find a friend's corpse the next day, after the enemy had bayoneted it for sport, and fueled in otherwise civilized men the spirit they needed to lay flame into caves, to call for napalm, to drop satchels of TNT onto men hiding in holes.

They had come again, as they come year after year, so that their friends could tell them that they did the only things they could have done. The reunion is an annual catharsis—a once-a-year opportunity to not only celebrate the past, but to grant each other absolution from it. Not from Guadalcanal or New Britain. From Peleliu.

It was more than just the bloodiest match of the distant and unfathomable Pacific campaign—"A living hell," Jesse Hollingsworth told me, "from start to finish." It was a betrayal of everyone involved. It was fought on a whim for an ego. To the critics of the decision to drop the atomic bomb, who trace the modern loss of faith in the nation's military to the twin mushroom clouds, the true historians of the Second World War will suggest they look one year farther back, to the landing on Peleliu, to find the seeds of the disillusion of the sixties, and the subsequent dissolution in which we're mired now.

There was no need to fight it, but fight it they did. And its legacy was everywhere I looked in the Riviera ballroom.

"We had a young kid," Elmer Miller tells me. "On Peleliu. A BAR [Browning automatic rifle] man. He got shot one night and we had to draw back. We had to leave him out there. Couldn't get his body until the next morning. He was all cut up. They'd jabbed him. Revenge."

Miller has come to sit next to Theron Cordray and Jack Parrish at the C-1-5 table. When I tell him what I'm doing, he says, "My kids don't know a damned thing." Elmer Miller tells me, although I don't ask, "I can't remember half of it, and the other half, the half I want to forget, I can't. What the hell is there to tell? The noncombatants—they're the ones who talk. The ones on the battlefield, they don't talk."

Elmer Miller speaks haltingly. On the left side of his

temple a depression in his skull begins at the side of his forehead and runs back to his ear, a furrow three inches long, left by a Japanese shell—a .31-caliber, he says. It took a piece of his ear, too. He got it on Peleliu.

He was unconscious for seven days. The same bullet that carved across the plane of his head without burrowing in went on to take out another marine in the jugular.

Miller doesn't really want to talk about Peleliu; he has been taking medication for years to forget about it. Eventually, though, he does talk. He has weighed the stakes, and has decided that he has to help me in what I am doing.

"There was four of us," he says. "One got killed right off the bat. Hit in the back of the head. It came out his mouth."

He pauses.

"You go through so goddamned much, you can't forget it. But you can't talk about it. It builds up. The different ones I saw killed. The different ones I saw with arms and legs missing."

Unlike his friends, Elmer is drinking a Coke. He tells me he hasn't had a drink in thirty years. When he first got out, he got drunk every night for six or seven months, and told nothing of anything to anyone. But he was having nightmares. So finally he started talking to his wife. Then he went to the V.A. hospital. The doctors diagnosed his ailment as epileptic seizures before they rediagnosed it as post-traumatic stress syndrome. Miller quit his job installing deep well pumps because he didn't want to be operating heavy machinery when he had the flashbacks.

Now Miller goes to the V.A. hospital once a month. He gets his medication to control the memories. He speaks to his counselor.

"He asks me brief questions," he tells me, "and I give

185

him brief answers—to keep the conversation going, is all.
At first they're interested in you. Now they want you in
and out. They got so many patients. They're forgetting the
war. There's guys in Washington don't know what the
war is."

I notice that he is crying. The tears are welling and slid-
ing down, gently, into the wrinkles of his face. Soundlessly.
We sit in silence for a long time. Perhaps minutes. Then
Elmer Miller says, "You know, a lot of guys like souvenirs." I remain silent. It seems like a non sequitur.

"I got a good souvenir," he says. "I got a good souvenir.
I got my life. That's the only souvenir I ever wanted. That's
the best one you could get."

He is blinking at the tears, and he stops them. They well
in his eyelids, but they no longer spill.

The flight from Port Moresby to Manila takes all night
because instead of stopping in Manila, the jet flies right
over the Philippines and up to Hong Kong first, where it
lands, then turns around and flies south again. This is like
flying to Chicago from New York by way of Denver. I am
not surprised. By now, I have grown accustomed to endless
flights over seamless stretches of ocean. Air travel in the
Pacific is like taking a train across the United States; it
takes so long that you resign yourself to a different internal
pace.

In Manila, I check into an airport hotel and go to sleep
in the early evening, only to be awakened in the middle of
the night by someone shaking my bed. No, I realize: it is
four men shaking my bed—one at each corner. But there's
no one there. Then I hear the brass handles on the dresser
clacking against the drawers, rhythmically, swaying, and I

understand that I am in the middle of an earthquake—
what must be a fairly serious one. I hear footsteps and
voices in the hallway. I lie in the bed and figure that in the
morning I will discover that the runways have been
churned open, and the airport will be closed for months. I
will be trapped in Manila. Then I do the most extraordinary thing: I fall back asleep. I do not dream of my father.

I hardly ever dream of my father—once every five years
or so—but I dreamt of him three times while I was looking
for his battlegrounds. In the first dream he showed up in
my office at home, and simply asked me, "Why would
you go back there?" He was talking about Guadalcanal. I
explained as best I could. He neither approved nor disap-
proved—wearing, instead, the tight-lipped expression that
appeared in all of the family's slides.

In the second dream my mother led me into a movie
theater. There was no movie on the screen, but people were
scattered in twos and threes throughout the theater. She
motioned for me to sit alone in an empty row. I took a
seat, and then turned around, and my father was sitting
alone in the row behind me. I understood in the dream
that he had come from wherever he was so that I could ask
him about my project. I told him I still intended to go back
to his islands to write a book. That I hadn't changed my
mind. He was silent, and looking at the movie screen, upon
which now played a film I don't recall. Finally he said that
if I was really going to go ahead with this, had I called his
old friend? And he gave me a name. In the dream I wrote
down the name. Then he got up and left the theater. Then
everyone in the theater got up and started to walk out, too.
My mother didn't seem in a hurry to catch him. I wondered
why she was letting him go. She told me we were all going
to a dinner for him, but when we got to the restaurant, he

187

wasn't there. Everyone there had come to celebrate him, and they all knew he wouldn't be there. I was the only one who didn't know he wasn't going to attend. He'd gone back to where he was supposed to be; I woke up knowing that very strongly. I had summoned him, or he had come on his own, from the place he was in now. I could not recall the name he'd given me.

In the third dream, about the time I finished the research for this book, he and I were drinking beer on someone's roof, as if it were something we did all the time.

In the morning I learned that while there had indeed been an earthquake, the runways were fine. The epicenter was seventy-five miles to the south. A tsunami washed an entire village on Mindanao into the sea.

Three hours east of Manila, dollops of jungle that looked like furry green mounds started to appear in the water beneath the Continental Micronesia 727: outlying atolls of the Palau chain. The jet banked and approached a small wet airstrip; the hills that flanked it rose sharply. They were impossibly green—Polynesian green.

I didn't know what to expect on Peleliu, or what to look for. I had a copy of the Marine Corps historical monograph under my arm, but by the time I had left, I had not heard from the Awards Division, so I didn't know if my father had won his Bronze Star on Peleliu. I did have a tourist guidebook that spoke highly of Palau's exotic birds.

In immigration two large dogs sniffed my luggage thoroughly. I had read that Palau was a widely known transit point for drug shipments heading from East Asia.

A NEW AGE DAWNS ON THE REPUBLIC OF PALAU'S JOURNEY AS A SOVEREIGN NATION read a sign on a large billboard next to the terminal. The nation of 9,000 natives and 6,000 foreign workers had become independent one month before my arrival. Palau had been a U.S. trust since the war. After a stormy recent relationship—the States wanted to allow nuclear-powered vessels to use the ports; Palau voted itself a nuclear-free nation in the seventies— in October of 1994 Palau voted to end the relationship. The USA handed over $200 million immediately, with the promise of $300 million more over the next fifteen years. Palau is now a free land. Tuna exports to Japan provide its most secure income. Forty thousand tourists from Asia annually visit the island chain in the middle of absolute nowhere. Its largest land mass is an island named Babelthuap, lying just north of Koror. Peleliu is the southernmost of fifty atolls.

Outside the terminal, at a corner of the runway, sat a pitted two-engine plane bearing the legend PARADISE AIR. A mechanic told me that they did indeed fly to Peleliu. There was a flight two hours hence. I was the only passenger on the plane.

The airstrip on Peleliu was short, made of crushed coral; on all sides, the jungle leaned in to frame it. There was no sign of the longer strip intended for our B-29s. It had been eaten by jungle.

As I stepped out of the plane, I detected a different fragrance to the Peleliu jungle. It has something to do with the ungiving white coral rock, which reflected the blistering sunlight and seemed to double its intensity. It was the fetid and fertile scent of a place where rain erupts in a fury in the late afternoon every day before the sun comes back to steam it away. It was a deep smell, the smell of the stew of spontaneous generation, as if the right lightning strike could breed life from the muck.

The Peleliu air terminal consisted of a wooden bench covered by a wooden roof. Beneath it stood a smiling man in a short-sleeved shirt, a plump man. His smile was a little like Peter Lorre's. Tangie Hesus met the plane every day. Tangie's aunt had a guesthouse in town, he said, and he had a van. He would be glad to give me tours.

"Our population is six hundred," Tangie told me as we wound our way up the crushed coral road; the trees wrapped the roadway completely, so that we were driving in a tunnel roofed by high branches. "They eat taro, bananas, papaya. They fish. They grow their own vegetables."

As we entered the village, we passed surprisingly modern and well-kept homes. They looked like a lower-middle-class neighborhood in Miami: pastel-colored cinder block, mold beneath the eaves. I saw modern motorcycles, and we passed an auto mechanic. I saw no gardens.

Tangie told me that he had a war museum. Tangie has made the battle of Peleliu a personal obsession. He guides tourists for a living, but the war is his first love. In the front yard of Tangie's aunt's house a large bent propeller from a fighter plane was stuck upright in the grass. The guest house comprised four empty bedrooms, a communal room, and a small kitchen. The bathroom, in a separate building, had no running water; a large drum of rainwater sat outside the hut.

The Peleliu War Museum was a small wooden building, and when I opened the door, the hot air leapt out, dry and dusty and fragrant of old things long undisturbed. A few dozen veterans had visited the island on the anniversary of

the attack two months earlier; I don't think the door had
been opened since.

There were photographs taken from Japanese corpses:
Of Manchuria. Of a beautiful young woman. Of a field of
sheep. There was a leaflet from the Japanese to the landing
marines:

> To Reckless Yankee Doodle. Do you know about the
> naval battle done by the American 58th fleet at the
> sea near Formosa and Philippine. Japanese powerful
> Air Force had sunk their 19 aeroplane carriers, 4 bat-
> tle ships, 10 several carriers and destroyers, along
> with sending 1,261 ship aeroplanes into the sea. From
> the result we think that you can imagine what shall
> happen next around Palau on you. WHAT IS PITY!!
> Must you sacrifice you pay. Thanks for you advice
> notes of surrender. Be we haven't any reason to sur-
> render, to those who are fated to be totally destroyed
> in a few days later. You shall get an very stern attack.
> We mean an cruel attack!!

I found a machine gun that looks like my father's. It was
a Japanese Nambu, a 6.5-millimeter. And then, unexpect-
edly, I came across something else Tangie had pinned to a
wall: a copy of Tom Lea's *Life* magazine cover. Amid the
faded shades of war clothing and weapons and muster
rolls, the red of the blood on the face of the marine with
half of a face is vivid. I had not seen it in thirty years, since
I found it in my father's trunk.

I took my notebook and sat on a bench outside of the
governor's office, which commanded a view of the school,
the basketball court, and a sign that read PALAU SAYS NO

TO DRUGS. The village was quiet except for the passing of the occasional pickup truck and, in the silence that followed each car, the song of the morning bird. The song was a series of seemingly random notes sung as if someone were blowing through a hollow reed. A chorus of other birds sang behind it, from a large hill that overlooked the school.

No one stopped to say hello to me. An old man waved. A child giggled. But no one between the age of ten and sixty looked me in the eye. I thought it odd that there were modern cars going up and down the crushed coral road, far more cars than circumstances would seem to call for. And while there may have been 600 people total on the island, and only a few hundred in the village proper, there were four grocery stores in the village. They stocked Doritos and Snickers and Gatorade. There were no farms to be seen, and few gardens. No fishing boats were moored anywhere I could see. There was no apparent means of sustenance, but cars were plentiful and radios and tape decks were everywhere, hoisted onto the shoulders of kids wearing shades. Motor scooters puttered on the road, too. Pink motor scooters.

Most of the men wore sunglasses. Most of the cars had tinted glass. Most of their drivers wore sunglasses. No one showed the slightest curiosity at the presence of a white man with a notebook. Something was wrong about Peleliu.

Then, something had been wrong about Peleliu from the start.

By September 1944, two years after the first marines had landed on Guadalcanal, the tide of the Pacific war had clearly turned. The marines were methodically pushing the

Japanese back up the face of the Pacific, island by island; the outcome was inevitable. But the deeper the marines reached into the Japanese sphere and pressed the emperor's best soldiers back toward their homeland, the more desperate the Japanese grew—and the tougher the fighting became, because of both the changing Japanese tactics and the dramatically changing battlefield terrain.

The Japanese troops had learned through two years of one-sided losses that blind banzai charges were not particularly effective, and had settled in to wage a war of attrition. The topography of the atolls of the central Pacific aided and abetted them—a point that was dramatically underscored in the fall of 1943, when the Second Marine Division was assigned the invasion of Betio, in the Tarawa chain of the Gilbert Islands, only to discover that fighting on an atoll of solid coral was nothing like waging a jungle campaign.

The landing on Tarawa was a bloodbath; the marine landing vehicles were hung up on a reef, and as the marines waded in to shore, they were butchered. The Japanese were dug well into the coral terrain; a slice of coral 800 yards wide cost the marines 800 lives—one life for every three feet of terrain. All of the 4,000 Japanese troops were killed.

Eight months later the marines hit Saipan, a clump of coral and rock in the Marianas chain to the northwest; here the stakes had increased dramatically. Saipan cost the marines 3,143 dead and 13,000 wounded. The heat, the lack of foliage, the sharp and brutal coral all made for a far more savage brand of fighting than anyone had anticipated.

By the time Douglas MacArthur proposed Operation Stalemate—suggesting that Peleliu be invaded in September 1944 to protect his right flank upon the occasion of his promised return to the Philippines, six hundred miles to the west—it was apparent that the Japanese defenses on the coral islands presented objectives far more difficult to fight for than those in the sand-and-mud jungles of Melanesia.

When the marines invaded the Solomons and Cape Gloucester, their enemy had been, for the most part, as inexperienced at jungle fighting as they were. In addition, the Japanese on Guadalcanal and New Britain had been in place only a short time. When the marines began landing on the islands to the northwest, out in the vast oceanic outback of the Pacific, they found an enemy that had been preparing for the invasions for, in some cases, as long as a year, and had mastered the harsh terrain.

In contemplating an invasion of Peleliu, the Allies apparently didn't understand well enough that Peleliu's terrain, while it lay close to both the Philippines and Melanesia, was nothing like the fertile muck of the lands they'd been fighting on heretofore; at the core of its soul, Peleliu was just another unforgiving chunk of razor-sharp coral rock. Reconnaissance photographs showed twelve square miles of hilly jungle. Peleliu was originally a coral-covered part of the ocean floor; it was shoved above the surface by volcanic action. The thin topsoil above the coral was capable of supporting only a scrub jungle, though from above, to the planes, it looked as thick as New Britain's.

The Navy thought it was bombarding jungle. In fact, it was scraping thin topsoil off solid coral. When that topsoil had been blasted away, nothing was visible, save a handful of two-story concrete buildings. Beneath the coral, unknown to the Allied command, was a city of 13,000 men —soldiers who had been blasting out elaborate caves, warrens capable of holding hundreds of men; in one case, more than 1,000.

They knew they were digging their graves. The commanding general, Colonel Kunio Nakagawa, had been instructed one month prior to the invasion, "Kill as many Americans as you can before the last Japanese soldier dies at his post."

"We are ready to die honorably," said Lieutenant General Sadae Inoue, at Koror, on July 11, 1944.

Operation Stalemate was set for September 15 under the command of Major General William H. Rupertus, the commander of the First Division. Rupertus was not highly thought of either in strategic terms or—equally important in a marine command—in terms of character and charisma. In 1929, when he was stationed in China, a scarlet-fever epidemic killed Rupertus's wife and his young son and daughter. He was said to have never recovered; by the time he was given the First Division after New Britain, he was humorless and demanding and introverted. His command of the forces at Peleliu was not considered to be a morale-booster among the troops.

The victory at Guadalcanal has been attributed in part to the personality of General Alexander Archer Vandegrift, then commander of the First Division, whose optimism and infectious good cheer filtered down to the lowliest PFC. William Rupertus commanded little respect, except from the man who commanded him—coincidentally, Vandegrift himself, who was by now the commandant of the United States Marine Corps. Rupertus's immediate superior was Major General Roy Geiger, the commander of the

III Marine Amphibious Corps, which included the First Marine Division. But it was Vandegrift who had installed Rupertus, his friend, and it was widely believed that Rupertus would succeed Vandegrift at the helm of the corps.

In the weeks prior to the planned invasion, Rupertus took his division off Pavuvu and back to Guadalcanal to practice landings—a move that could not have made the First Division happy; they had no good memories of Guadalcanal. Further ominous overtones: Rupertus fractured his ankle in the landing exercises. And then Rupertus did an extraordinary thing: he called in his various commanders and told them to tell the troops that the Peleliu invasion was going to take two or three days—"a tough quickie"—which made him look rather foolish two months into a battle whose casualty rates were not only unacceptable but appalling.

Worse, the campaign served no strategic purpose whatsoever.

The capriciousness with which the Peleliu campaign was waged—and history's determination to erase the island's name from the war—is more easily understood with a small amount of background.

In May 1944, as the marines left New Britain, Douglas MacArthur made a pitch to keep the First Marine Division in the Army, as the advance assault troops for his Sixth Army's planned march back through the Philippines on his way to Tokyo. Admiral Chester Nimitz, the commander of all naval forces in the Pacific, of course wanted the First back where it belonged, in the Navy. Ultimately, Admiral Ernest King, the chief of naval operations and a member of the Joint Chiefs of Staff, ordered MacArthur to give the marines back immediately.

Soon afterward Nimitz began to formulate a plan of his own, one that was quite different from that which the Joint

Chiefs had planned. In July, Franklin Roosevelt agreed to meet with Nimitz. Roosevelt convinced MacArthur to fly in from Australia, and the three held a conference in Hawaii. Nimitz recommended bypassing the Philippines entirely: save lives and time by mounting a direct assault, as big as that of Normandy, on the home islands of Japan. MacArthur wanted to do it his way; we could not betray the Filipinos, he said.

After three days, Roosevelt decided to let MacArthur have his way; in addition, he exacted from Nimitz a vow that the admiral would do everything he could to support MacArthur. Roosevelt's decision represented a bitter defeat for Nimitz, who nonetheless told his staff that everything would be done to support the plan. Operation Stalemate was a go.

On the military front, though, mitigating factors intruded as the assault date drew near. Several months earlier, in March, a naval task force had attacked Peleliu and destroyed some 250 Japanese planes, either on the ground or in the air, significantly weakening the Japanese air strength. Now, in the weeks prior to the Peleliu invasion, another naval action revealed that Japanese influence in this part of the Pacific had been severely crippled. Vice Admiral William F. "Bull" Halsey's Third Fleet had decimated Samar Island in the Philippines, and was surprised at the lack of Japanese resistance. At that point, for all practical purposes, it became apparent that there was no Japanese naval air presence in the Pacific at all; the American fleet could roam with impunity.

Halsey had also noted, after his attacks on the Philippines, that while MacArthur was planning to land on Mindanao, to the south in the Philippines, there was no Japanese presence on Leyte, far to the north. The purpose of invading Peleliu would be to secure the airfield so that the Japanese air power could not threaten MacArthur. But there was no Japanese airpower to threaten anyone; what was left of it lay in wreckage on Peleliu's six-thousand-foot coral airstrip.

"The American fleet could go almost anywhere in the Pacific without any significant challenge," historian Harry A. Gailey has written. "We controlled the air; we controlled the sea lanes. The danger was extreme for any Japanese ship plying the waters south of Japan."

Just before the invasion of Peleliu, then, Bull Halsey called his staff together, including Harold Stassen, his assistant chief of staff. "I'm going to stick my neck out . . . upset many applecarts, possibly all the way to Mr. Roosevelt and Mr. Churchill," Stassen quoted Halsey to the late Bill D. Ross, author of *Peleliu: Tragic Triumph*.

Just before the assault, Halsey sent word to Nimitz recommending that Stalemate be scrapped: bypass Peleliu, move up MacArthur's invasion of Leyte, and give MacArthur the First Marine Division, as he'd wanted, to spearhead his attacks as he moved toward the Japanese homeland.

Nimitz passed Halsey's recommendation on to the Joint Chiefs, who were meeting with Roosevelt and Churchill in Quebec at the time, but he altered the proposal: he excluded Halsey's recommendation that Peleliu be bypassed. The Joint Chiefs approved Nimitz's proposal. Leyte's invasion would be moved up. But Peleliu would still be invaded. Nimitz never publicly or privately revealed why he did not pass on to Roosevelt Halsey's recommendation to bypass Peleliu.

Stassen, who was to be Eisenhower's ranking military advisor on the White House staff for three years, told Ross,

"The invasion of Peleliu was a terrible mistake, a tragedy that was needless and should not have happened."

The preinvasion Naval bombardment was supposed to last three days, but it was called off after two. All of the targets had been hit. But the targets were nothing but coordinates on a map. When the island had been thoroughly shelled, and every grid had been hit, no enemy movement could be seen, so on the third day all was silent. The next morning the silence was broken by the shelling that preceded the landing. After the shelling stopped, as the LSTs (landing transport) headed for the reef, there was no sound from the enemy. The island appeared dormant and empty.

"I remember telling the guys on the boat that we'd be back by nightfall," Francis Liebermann recalls. Liebermann was a first lieutenant in the 1-5.

The island was entirely denuded. Splintered stumps stood where trees had been. The coral looked like bone. One of my father's men told me that when he watched Neil Armstrong land on the moon, he was instantly reminded of the terrain on Peleliu.

"It was nothing but a mass of smoke—you couldn't see the beach," said Jesse Hollingsworth, another lieutenant in the 1-5. "You couldn't see anything. The guys in the boat were saying, 'Oh boy—this is going to be easy.'

"But I remember watching this one marine plane. That sucker dove into those clouds of smoke and pulled up to come out and his wing went off. I said, 'Uh-oh. They got something down there.' "

The LSTs opened up and disgorged the first amtracks onto the reef, one hundred yards out—and the island erupted with the sound of Japanese artillery. The first wave was getting blown out of the water. And the second, a minute and a half later. And the third, a minute and a half after that.

"The amtrack on either side of me," Bob Amery said, "got blown out of the water by direct hits."

Amtracks were flipping over in the water. The ones that made it to the beach were taking direct mortar hits. Not only had the Japanese targeted every square inch of the reef with their artillery, they had covered every bit of the beach with their mortars. And just inside the beach, they had mined the coral.

When the marines reached the beaches on the western shore of the southern half of the island, all they could do was squat behind the wrecked amtracks and dive into the shell holes.

"It was the worst landing in the war," Bill Looney told me. "That was the worst in the war. The whole war.

"I had a brand new corpsman ask me some time during the first day if this was as tough as some of the others," Looney said. The corpsman was worried that if this were just routine, then what was a really tough landing going to be?

"You can mark it down," Looney told him. "This is the toughest."

"The shit hit the fan," Jake Omdahl said. "It was unbelievable. It was a Chinese fire drill. It was a horrible thing."

"Horrible" wasn't a word I'd heard often from my father's men, but I heard it a lot when they were talking about Peleliu.

"It was a really horrible situation," Bill Hunsicker told me. "I was horrified. It was pretty horrifying. You didn't know what was going to happen one instant to the next. You just hoped you'd be one of the lucky ones. An awful lot of my friends weren't lucky. I've tried to forget it. I've really tried to forget it.

"I was scared half to death. I think everybody else was, too."

That was another word I'd never heard any of them use: "scared."

Most of them told me they'd done everything they could to simply obliterate the memory of Peleliu from their minds. Jake Omdahl told me that until six years ago he remembered none of it. Only when one of his sons wrote off to the Awards Department of the Navy for his father's medals did Omdahl begin to stir up some of the memories.

"It was too painful," he said. "The memories were too painful. At least I was able to open my mind to talk about it. I didn't want to talk about it before then. All of my friends felt the same way. It's a funny thing. I guess you couldn't handle it. Even when we met amongst each other after the war, we didn't."

I asked him what the medals were.

"I dunno, a half-dozen of 'em," he said. "I don't know what they are."

I believed him.

I found no one who could remember my father at the landing on Peleliu. For the most part, I was told, it was chaos. The First Regiment to the north, the Fifth in the middle, the Seventh to the south—no one was worried about sticking with their outfits. They were trying to stay alive. They couldn't dig into the coral; they had to find shell holes or mine holes and scrabble down behind the rubble. They huddled behind disabled amtracks—the Buffaloes, with their armament and guns, and the Alligators, with no armament at all. The beach was a graveyard for the landing vehicles.

"We almost got pushed back into the sea," Lou Schott recalls. Schott had a platoon of 44 men under his command when he landed. When he left, with mortar shrapnel in his arm, he had 6.

"I remember one guy. I remember his pant leg was wet. 'I don't think a man can have the shit scared out of him,' he said to me, 'but he sure as hell can have the piss scared out of him.' "

The Fifth Marines were not getting the worst of it. To their left, Chesty Puller's First Marines were getting slaughtered. The plan called for Puller's First to take out the Japanese in the hills north of the airfield, allowing the Fifth to take the airfield. But where the First Marines had landed, the Japanese controlled a point that stood on higher ground. No one could take them out. A more diligent and conscientious preinvasion shelling plan might have taken out any pieces of geography that could have given the Japanese such an advantage. The point could have been wiped off the map. But it wasn't, and the men of the First Marine Regiment were dying at an unacceptable rate. Peleliu represented the nadir of Chesty Puller's marine career; within a few weeks he would be relieved of his command, so excessive were the First Regiment's casualties.

None of the men in the Fifth had the luxury of giving thought to the men on their flank. They were scrambling for every yard. The airfield lay a few hundred yards away. The Japanese were defending it from the high ground. The Fifth Marines would gain a few hundred yards through the afternoon, at most; other estimates put their gains at seventy yards: less than the length of a football field for a full day's fighting.

It was during the first afternoon that one of the 1-5

earned the only Congressional Medal of Honor the battalion would be awarded during the Pacific war. A boy named Carlton Rouh picked it up. He and my father were friends, Jake Omdahl told me. Omdahl was Rouh's commanding officer. He sent Rouh up to the observation post, and the next thing he knew, Rouh was walking back to the beach, holding his gut.

"The Japs came out of the ground all over the post," Omdahl remembers. "One came out and threw a grenade out and he leapt for it, to throw it back, whatever. Kind of a natural instinct. It hit him hard. He walked back to the beach—it was fifty yards or so—holding his gut."

Francis Liebermann was with my father and Colonel Boyd on the beach when Boyd called regiment headquarters. Liebermann remembers my father standing by as Boyd radioed headquarters.

"Boyd said, 'We're getting decimated down here,' " Liebermann said. "I remember that word: decimated."

The temperature reached 120 degrees. Except for North Africa, conditions for Peleliu's invasion represented the worst of any battle in the war. It was so hot, Bob Amery remembers, that if you touched metal it would burn you. You had to be careful about where you touched your own weapon.

By the end of the afternoon the 1-5 had advanced as far as an abandoned Japanese tank trap, where they hoped to wait out the night, but it was not to be. At dusk the marines heard the shouts of the Japanese on their radio frequencies: "We drink marine blood!" and the more conventional "Banzai"—at which point, to their amazement, a wave of Japanese tanks began to pour toward them across the airfield. The Japanese had decided to try and push the marines back into the sea with a counteroffensive.

"Of all the things we were looking for, a tank attack was the last thing we expected," Ray Fenton said.

A remarkable sight greeted the marines nearly delirious from the lack of drinking water and the insufferable heat: Japanese troops had strapped themselves to the sides and tops of the tanks. Others were running alongside. They were blowing trumpets. It was an insane assault; apparently the Japanese hoped to push the marines back off the island by striking such fear into the hearts of the marines with their bushido bravery that the marines would turn tail and run. As was often the case with Japanese battlefield strategy, the notion was impressive in bravado, if entirely ineffective.

"They came right across the airfield," Ray Fenton said. "They had their little tin trumpets and their little tin tanks. They were beautiful targets. Lot of confusion. A lot of smoke. They ran over more people than they did anything else."

"They went right through our lines," Whiskey Williams said. Whiskey was a first lieutenant in the A-1-5. "I think they were doped up with sake. They were strapped onto the tanks. They'd always do things like that. They'd have a guy strap a land mine to his chest and run into a tank."

"Somebody yelled, 'Hey, here they come!'—and here comes about thirty tanks," Bob Amery told me. "I read afterward they found nineteen, but I didn't believe it. It was the biggest bunch of tanks I ever saw."

The Japanese had supported the tanks with mortar and artillery fire, Amery recalls, and the last thing he wanted to do was get out of his foxhole. But when his company commander told him to go back to the beach to find more machine-gun ammunition, he was in no position to argue. He scampered back, taking some troops with him, looking for ammo.

"I'm hoping to see a nice big pile of machine-gun ammunition," Amery said. "What we did find was a bunch of dead marines. We took their cartridge belts. Then someone had a bright idea: 'Look at all these knocked-out Buffaloes —they got a machine gun in them.' So I climbed down into one. The operator was splattered all over the inside of the thing. Somebody found a wrench and tools, and we uncoupled the .50-caliber gun from the Buffalo and our safari went back up there with a .50, just in time—the last Jap tank was still running around."

All of the Japanese troops had been slaughtered. A few of the tanks got through the lines.

Fenton recalls the tank charge as less than intimidating. Jesse Hollingsworth remembers it differently.

"I was scared for my life," he said. He'd jumped into a shell hole and watched a camouflaged tank moving toward him and his men. The hole was big enough that the tank would land in it, he remembers. But it missed.

"The thing went by. The most we could do was lob some grenades. When it went by, our tanks had just landed. Everyone in the world started shooting at that thing. They started piling out of the top. I remember the first guy piling out of there. I don't know how many times he got hit."

In a nearby shell hole, Bernard Boutelier and Francis Liebermann watched one of the tanks heading full speed straight for their position.

"What are we going to do?" Boutelier asked. "Nothing

we can do, except hope they run over us, or turn around,"
Liebermann said. They huddled, transfixed, waiting for the
tank to come right into the hole, until they heard the boom
of an American 75-millimeter gun.

"Turns out we had a Sherman about seventy-five feet
away," Liebermann said. "Its tread had been blown, so it
couldn't move, but its turret worked. They put a 75 shell
right into the tank and it burned all night. We could smell
the burning flesh. It furnished a pretty good light."

History would record that Peleliu was the battle where the
Japanese started to abandon the senseless bravado style
of fighting, as Ross explained in *Peleliu: Tragic Triumph:*
"The Japanese on Peleliu were just as willing to die for
their country as any the marines had ever met. But at long
last they had learned the futility of dying merely for the
sake of dying. Whatever we had been up against before,
we were taking on the enemy varsity now."

But there can be no explanation save "dying for the sake
of dying" for the tank assault. The enemy force was 400
to 500 men, later identified as Colonel Nakagawa's best
troops, veterans of the Manchuria campaign. When it
was over, there were 450 dead Japanese, and while it may
have been that the Japanese honestly believed that the
tanks and infantry would wipe out the Fifth Marines, any
hope for a Japanese victory dwindled when, at the first
artillery and bazooka attacks from the marines, the Japanese vehicles began to race across the airstrip, leaving their
infantry behind, which doomed both the men and the
tanks.

Ray Fenton was a second lieutenant in the A-1-5. His
first—and last—afternoon on Peleliu featured an encoun-

ter with bushido at its most dramatic. Advancing toward the airfield, Fenton heard an explosion behind him and took a piece of shrapnel in the back of the neck. He figures it was either an enemy mortar or a short round from our navy.

"We never objected to [the short rounds]; at least they were close to our front," Fenton said. "We were glad to have it as close as they could get it. Besides—we used to blame the Navy for it because we blamed the Navy for everything. Like taking us places we didn't want to go."

Fenton walked back to the beach, where a corpsman put a bandage on his neck, not knowing that a piece of shrapnel an inch and a half long had dug its way inside.

The beach was a mess, Fenton remembers; the First Marine casualties were pouring in. There was nothing for him to do but wait to be evacuated. But late in the afternoon, when he heard that there was going to be a tank attack, he went back to the front.

"Being young and eager, and having lived with these guys, I went back up to the line," Fenton said. But his neck had started bleeding again, and he was growing light-headed and dizzy. He started back to the beach. He remembers picking up a tommy gun from a dead marine. The tommy gun was a prize weapon. The rifles the marines had been issued were .30-caliber carbines—tinny weapons, Fenton recalls; they were good for hunting rifles—"but we weren't interested in marksmanship. We wanted a lot of lead in front of us." The .45-caliber pistol at his side, Fenton recalls, "was good for throwing at people."

So Fenton was slogging his way to the back, his tommy gun slung over his shoulder, dazed from his wound and weakened; the shrapnel had lodged a millimeter away from his spinal cord. Suddenly the coral ground moved, and up out of a spider hole jumped a Japanese major, followed by two unarmed enlisted men. The major had a sidearm and his sword. If the major had used his gun, Fenton would have been dead. But instead the major screamed "Banzai," and from fifteen feet away charged with his samurai sword.

"I don't know why," he says now. "They kind of loved to die in battle, I guess. I guess 'banzai' might look good on the death certificates. Anyway, I had a lot of blood flowing around. I was probably a little woozy and running on adrenaline . . . he comes running across. I lift the carbine and pull the trigger." The carbine jammed.

The major reached Fenton, lunged with his sword, hit the front of Fenton's helmet and opened a deep cut in his forehead. Fenton backed off, swung the machine gun up from his hip, and pressed the trigger. "I kind of cut him in two. The men behind him got some of his bullets."

I asked Fenton if he could remember what it was like to kill the men.

"I didn't feel anything you'd feel as if you'd killed a person," he told me. "At that point, to us, they were little more than bloodthirsty monkeys. They would decapitate prisoners and torture them. They were ruthless in their whole conduct. I had no feeling other than I was so darned busy trying to stay alive. I don't remember what his face looked like except his mouth was open yelling 'Banzai.'

"I have no moral concerns, I guess. They probably didn't think of us as people, either. I guess you could say the Geneva Convention didn't get that far."

Fenton picked up the samurai sword and took it with him back to the beach, where he was patched up and sent home. I asked him if he still had the sword. He said he didn't. He said that after the war, when the relatives of the slain Japanese appealed for the swords to be returned, Fenton returned his.

The Fifth's orders for the first day had been to take the airfield, which lay some three hundred yards in from the beach, but they were unable to reach it. The First had been unable to get the Japanese out of the ridges north of the airfield, so the Japanese had no trouble covering the field. The marines dug in for the night.

The same day, MacArthur's Sixth Army landed unopposed on the Philippines.

On Day One 92 marines were killed and 1,148 wounded.

They spent the night in the trenches, without water. Each man had had two canteens full when he landed. No water would be brought until the following day, when it arrived in gasoline tanks that hadn't been washed out, and when the marines drank from the drums, they fell sick by the dozens. It was several days before someone realized that the water table lay just below the island's surface; fresh drinking water could have been flowing from the start if wells had been dug.

No one slept the first night. Sleeping was a dereliction of duty. The marine's first concern was the other marine.

The late George P. Hunt wrote a book about Peleliu called *Coral Comes High*. Hunt was in Chesty Puller's First. Hunt won the Navy Cross for his actions on the first night on Peleliu. His company, 240 at the landing, was reduced to 34. It killed 422 Japanese in three counterattacks.

George Hunt wrote a passage about the possible ways a marine could be killed in battle: ". . . still another, feeling no alertness, and allowing himself to be overcome with fatigue and being a slouch of a man, may fall asleep and meet a dreadful end on the point of a bayonet. That man betrays himself as well as his friends."

Walking back up the road from the museum, I saw a white woman leaving the school. I introduced myself. Roberta Passage was in her thirties, a Peace Corps volunteer from northern California. She invited me to sit down in the back yard of her house, across the road from the school.

"Sometimes you think of a place and you just want to go there," she told me. "I liked the idea of living on an island. I wanted to go somewhere sunny. Somewhere you could see the sun rise. And the sun set."

There were eight volunteers in the Palau program to which she'd been assigned. Six were slated for Babelthuap, one for the island of Angaur, and one for Peleliu. Roberta wanted Peleliu, and the Peace Corps, she said, wanted a woman on Peleliu this time. The previous two volunteers had been men, she told me, and the natives thought they were DEA agents.

"I wasn't the biggest party-er in our group," she said. "Peleliu is a big party state. There's more money here. They knew there was a lot of pot-smoking here, and they didn't want anyone irresponsible.

"I didn't have a clue until recently," she told me. "There was a big raid."

It was the first I'd heard of the marijuana and the DEA. Perhaps it helped to explain the dogs, the grocery stores, the cars. The attitude.

She told me that when the agents from Peleliu's own drug squads had come in to raid the island recently, everyone was wondering how they'd found the marijuana fields. There was talk of a white man with curly dark hair walking in the mountains just prior to the raid. Terrific, I said —I have curly dark hair and I'm here to climb in the hills. I was hoping she'd tell me not to worry. She didn't.

Roberta told me she didn't want to talk about the pot anymore. The journalist in me wanted to press her, but her term was to last another eight months, and she didn't want to endanger her relations. In fact, I was certain she didn't want to be seen talking to me as I wrote things down. During the hour we spoke, I noticed a native man watching me from across the road, sitting on a bench in the schoolyard. He had wild, frizzy hair, and he was wearing a camouflage jacket. Clearly he figured I was a drug agent interviewing Roberta about what she might know.

Roberta Passage had a particular sadness to her for someone who had come to where she always wanted to be —an island paradise.

"Considering everything I wanted out of life, I feel really lucky to be here," she told me. "When the sun comes out, the place is so beautiful."

But when I asked her how she got along with the natives, she thought for a moment and could not be enthusiastic.

"They separate themselves from people sometimes . . . I think Palauans, especially on Peleliu, there's a feeling of . . . braggadocio. They're clannish. And they're so gossipy."

In the evening, with nothing to do, I walked to the basketball court next to the school. A half-dozen boys were playing a game; a few more sat on the side. One was wearing sunglasses in the dark. They regarded me without expression. I waited a few moments, then approached one, and showed him a book I had about the war on Peleliu, and told him what I was doing. He nodded, looked at me, looked at the book, and walked away.

Parked behind the basket was a late-model Toyota pickup with shaded windows out of which issued the tooth-grinding thump of rock and roll through an expensive sound system. The rear window of the cab featured a United States Marine Corps emblem.

By the light of the marines' first dawn on Peleliu it was obvious that Chesty Puller's First had been unable to get off the point, so the coral mountain ranges north of the airfield were still full of Japanese.

The caves that weren't full of infantry featured the largest artillery the marines had ever seen: 200-millimeter mortars on rails, behind steel doors. They'd roll out, fire, and roll back in, and the doors would be closed. At the foot of the hills stood the Japanese headquarters, a two-story concrete fortress with massive steel doors. The airfield lay silent and already baking in the dawn.

At 8 A.M., word came through that, despite the First Regiment's inability to dislodge the Japanese from the hills above the exposed airfield, the Fifth Regiment was going to cross the airfield as planned. The mortars on rails were going to be aimed at them. In a moonscape, on an island stripped nude of foliage, reduced to coral rubble. Without water.

Most of the men who crossed the airfield that morning remember it as the worst moment of their war.

The field wasn't entirely bare; it was pockmarked with

shell holes from the initial naval bombardment, and littered with Japanese planes caught in the bombardment from the previous March and the carcasses of the Japanese tanks from the day before.

The first wave came out of the trench—and the hills erupted with artillery, mortar, and machine-gun fire. New, huge shell holes opened up: the giant Japanese mortars were in operation. Mortar shells fell from the sky. The field was raked in a constant enfilade of bullets.

"I ran into Low-Butt Stanley at Quantico years later," Jay Henry Gustafson recalled. "He said, 'I was scared to death, but I saw you running across, and I thought if you could do it, I could do it.' "

Russ Clay's squad was eight men strong when they landed on Peleliu, and two after they crossed the airfield. Clay crossed with his friend Duzzie. They got pinned halfway across. They dove into two bomb craters separated by an island of coral. Every time they tried to get out of the craters, the bullets would rake the strip of coral.

"You could hear it if somebody got it," Russ Clay told me. "It was like a 'plop' inside them. You could hear the bullets going through them. I shoot blackbirds with a BB gun, and it's the same sound. Like a soft plop. If you heard that, you knew somebody got it, and you'd want to get out of there."

On the other side of the field, Clay told me, he and Duzzie dove into a ditch. A Japanese mortar landed on Duzzie's side.

"Duzzie's brains were on my jacket," he said. "A terrible thing."

213

Later, I would find the muster roles of the 1-5. PFC Stephen S. Dosenczuk. That was Duzzie.

Russ Clay's tone was matter-of-fact, objective. He was looking for ways to describe what happened, and these were the words he came up with. It was not the first time I heard a marine describe a buddy's death in dispassionate terms, but I never heard it until they were talking about Peleliu.

Jesse Hollingsworth told me that crossing the airfield reminded him of a John Wayne movie: "You'd go as far as you could, then you'd hit the deck."

Hollingsworth figured he was hallucinating when he saw a Confederate flag lying outside of a shell hole. Then he looked in, and saw John Dusenberry, a captain in the A-1-5. Dusenberry was a legend; in the group photograph of the volleyball players on Pavuvu, Dusenberry is the cockiest of the bare-chested men, his hands on his hips, challenging the camera.

"He was hit," Hollingsworth remembered. "He had that Confederate flag—the same Confederate flag he hoisted on Shuri Castle on Okinawa. And—this is the truth—he had a quart of whiskey with him in the shell hole.

" 'They're going to evacuate me,' he said. 'Anybody who comes into this hole gets a drink.'

"So I took a slug."

At the other side of the airfield Hollingsworth jumped into the ditch with Whiskey Williams when a mortar shell landed in the hole. Both men were knocked out.

"When I came to, it might have been seconds, it might have been minutes," Hollingsworth said. "I looked at Whiskey Willy. I couldn't get him to wake up. There was blood coming out of his mouth. I popped my butt out of there and started counting survivors."

Hollingsworth reported that Williams had been killed. Hollingsworth was wrong. At least that's what Williams told me.

Williams said he remembered the bullets coming from the rear as he crossed the airfield. When he turned, he saw that the Japanese had sneaked in during the evening and taken up positions in their own destroyed aircraft.

"They shot us all to pieces," Whiskey Williams told me. "When I landed, I had two hundred fourteen men. After we crossed the airfield, I could account for only ninety-plus men."

That was after he woke up, bleeding through the mouth. Whiskey Willy said a fragment of shell had gone through his jaw, and that was where that blood was from.

"We were always told not to hide in a ditch," Williams said. "But they had us covered with so many small arms that we had to."

Whiskey Willy got the name because he was a teetotaler from eastern Tennessee until the division hit Melbourne. Even Williams had to go on a bender on Australia. Thereafter, he was Whiskey Willy Williams.

The march across the airfield, my father's men told me, was so terrifying that it claimed a share of psychological casualties. "Irvin Cleveland cracked up crossing the airfield," Lou Schott told me. "He started running up toward the high ground yelling, 'You bastards!' That did two things. First, he's exposing himself. Then, he's exposing our position. I went out and tackled him. They had to evacuate him. He never came back."

Halfway across the airfield a cry went up that the marines never thought they'd hear: "Gas!" Most of them had landed with gas masks but had thrown them away and filled their space with more essential supplies: cigarettes, toilet paper. When Bob Amery heard that a gas attack had begun, he considered it the final straw.

"I was so tired, and hot, and scared," Amery told me. "I figured, 'This is it. I'm on my way.' I wet my handkerchief with water and put it over my face, lay down and said, 'I'll lay here and die.' "

But there was no gas. They were just shells with colored smoke, so the Japanese could get a bead on the accuracy of their barrage.

After the Fifth had crossed the airfield, they holed up in a wide Japanese trench. The mortars had taken their toll. The Fifth's casualties were heavy. The regiment had faced an inverted horseshoe-shaped coral ridge with sheer, jagged peaks a few hundred feet high. The marines were down at the open end. The Japanese were holed up in the bottom of the horseshoe. Jesse Hollingsworth hoped his platoon wouldn't be ordered into the heart of the horseshoe—the Umurbrogol Range. He was relieved when he was told to go to the right and climb the hills from behind.

"We had a hell of a time getting up there because of the coral—it'll cut your guts out," he told me.

They climbed the ridge only to discover that Japanese snipers had the range if any of the marines stuck their heads over the top of the coral. The Japanese had field glasses, and their snipers could put a bullet right through your head at a hundred yards. Hollingsworth ordered his men to pile up spare bits of coral, to furnish peepholes at the snipers across the ridge.

"So when we got up, there was a dead marine," he told me. "One of us. I had been through a lot—you got to do your job—but we couldn't stay on that ridge with that dead body. That was the only time I ever had a problem with the men. I asked for volunteers. I didn't get any. 'He's one of us,' they said. 'We can't throw him off.'

"Now I had to do it. I had to get that body off of there. I was angry at the outfit that had left him up there. The stretcher-bearers couldn't get up there. I had a runner named Holmes. I said, 'We're going to do it.' And we threw it off.

"That Hollingsworth did such a thing—it's a memory I could never get over," Jesse Hollingsworth said.

It was while the Fifth was on the ridges that the Navy planes began dropping their bombs on the center of the horseshoe. My father was standing on one of the ridges.

They were the shortest bombing runs in the history of warfare: the base of the inverted horseshoe where the Japanese were holed up in the caves was no more than a hundred yards from the end of the airstrip. The American planes took off and dropped their bombs in the same maneuver.

"It was something to watch those planes," Hollingsworth said. "We used to say you could tell if a pilot was married or single. The single guys would stay low. The married guys would pull up quicker."

When I'd first asked Whiskey Williams if he knew my father, he said, "The Green Hornet! He got it on that ridge, got hit by the napalm!"

No, I said. He lived through Peleliu.

"That's right! It didn't get him!" Whiskey said immediately. Whiskey speaks in exclamations.

I had to ask: It almost did get him?

"He had a group of marines on one of the hills," Whiskey told me, "and they dropped a napalm bomb, and it liked to hit him. He skedaddled out of there. He was a brave little man."

Apparently, Whiskey Williams didn't know the original derivation of my father's nickname. Williams always thought it referred to his speed.

"He was awfully fast to be able to outrun a napalm bomb."

Retired Lieutenant General John McLaughlin recalled my father on that ridge.

"At Peleliu," McLaughlin wrote me, "I remember very well, when we were heavily engaged at the south end of the island in assaulting enemy positions in cliffs with lots of cave positions, that Major Tom Richmond came forward and worked with us company commanders in taking those very strongly held positions. We were assisted by tanks which I understand Tom had been instrumental in arranging, as I had lost a good many wonderful young marines in our earlier attacks."

McLaughlin told me he remembered working the caves in the south end of the ridge, and being told that Richmond was up on the top of the ridge, probably dropping satchels of explosives into the caves.

He was always out front, they told me. Apparently, on Peleliu, he was on top.

Tangie Hesus told me he had to set traps for the coconut crabs that lived in the caves in the Umurbrogol Range, to catch food for a party the village was having in a couple of days for the people on Babelthuap. Every year they welcomed the people of Babelthuap because the Babelthuap natives had taken them in during the battle fifty years ago, while the Americans and the Japanese were defoliating their homeland. Tangie told me he'd drop me at Orange One, the beach on which my father landed.

If the Japanese pillbox hadn't been planted on the southern end of the crescent, Orange One would be a beach from the imagination. The pillbox was perfectly round, like a water tank atop an urban apartment tower, and rusted to a brownish-orange. I began to walk toward it, only vaguely aware of the heat.

Unlike the sand of the Solomons and PNG, the sand on Orange One was white and fine. Polynesian sand. The beach wound around a crescent bay; palm fronds and shallow-rooted pine branches drooped over the beach, giving shade to the sand crabs. It was so quiet that after Tangie's van disappeared, I could hear the clacking of their tiny claws. In the sun the heat felt solid enough to reach out and touch.

A hundred yards offshore, on the other side of the light-blue lagoon, waves broke on the reef. The water between the reef and the beach was only a few feet deep. A bird with a long neck waded into the water to fish for the fish that darted in and out of the sea grass, which waved in the shallows like long green eyelashes. The water was so clear that at one point, when I thought I was still walking on sand, I suddenly found myself ankle-deep in water that was nearly as warm as the air.

As I stepped a few more feet into the water, the sole of my foot found something that didn't belong on a sea floor. I looked down to see that I was standing on a piece of a chassis of an amtrack. The frame of the amtrack fanned out like a steel skeleton. The differential gear was visible, which meant that the vehicle was upside down: It had taken a direct hit.

As I stood on it, motionless, a couple of small fish began to poke their heads out from beneath the rusted beams, and then more, and then a few more, until within a minute the six-inch deep water was full of them—fish with horizontal stripes, fish with vertical stripes like zebras, bright red fish. The devastated amtrack had provided the ideal reef for the kind of fish that tourists flock to see.

I resumed my walk in the white sun and silence; I could hear the beat of my heart in my ears—the pillbox at the end of the beach appeared to be getting no closer. I needed to rest. I sat down to rest on a large spool of rusted communication wire, three feet in diameter. It looked as if it had never been unwound. The rust and the decay made it seem like it belonged on the beach; I had thought it was a rock as I'd approached from a distance. Perhaps the radio man was killed on the beach. Perhaps they never needed it.

I sat down. Out of the corner of my eye I could see the black and brown land crabs scuttling away. They were like stars in the night sky: as soon as you tried to look at them directly, they weren't there.

The whole island was beginning to feel as if it was watching me, and waiting for me to go away.

The air began to feel superheated. I could wave my hand and feel the heat in it, as if I'd opened an oven and reached in. Two times on my walk to the pillbox I waded into the shallows and lay in the water, but this brought little relief. It had never occurred to me that the elements could be so integral a part of the Pacific campaign. The winters of the Russian front were common knowledge; the astounding heat of the South Pacific has long been ignored.

Finally I reached the pillbox. The floor was a few inches of the water, illuminated by sunlight from the outside. Its only opening faced to the rear. There were no open spaces or gun slots facing the direction from which the marines would have invaded. I could not imagine why.

I walked back up the beach, and as I reached my original starting point, a bus was winding its way down the trail, then pulled up near the beach. A dozen Taiwanese men piled out. Another dozen stayed in their seats, and leaned out the windows of the bus.

The native driver sidled over to me.

"Too much talking," he said to me, and nodded at his passengers, pantomiming a yapping jaw with his hand.

One of them was wearing a T-shirt bearing an English legend. "Hello," he said to me. He explained that he was from Los Angeles, and that the men with him made up a group from Taiwan who were interested in investing in a golf club and resort up on the island of Babelthuap.

One of them was speaking Chinese to the rest. I asked the English-speaking one what the man was saying.

"He is telling them that the water here turned red with the blood of the American soldiers."

It sounded like something someone had read. But then I looked at the lagoon, and the reef, and how shallow the water was, and it occurred to me that it might have literally been true.

I told the man that my father was a marine. That my father landed on this beach.

"He die here?"

No, I said.

"Lucky man!" he answered. "Lucky man!"

I walked fifty yards farther north, up the beach to where the First Marine Regiment had landed. Several rusted plates of steel lay on the sand and in the shallows. By now they seemed almost organic; they had somehow rusted to a color that blended with the flora.

Behind me, the men from the bus were howling with laughter. One of them had a dozen of the rest of them in stitches: he was pantomiming a hand-to-hand battle between two soldiers. He was pantomiming a man bludgeoning another with the butt of a rifle. Then he pantomimed a man bayoneting another man, in a goofy slapstick way. I watched them. This went on for a ridiculously long time, a full minute or more, until it seemed like some kind of theater. I wondered how people could laugh so long at something.

Tangie returned to pick me up, bearing a quart of Gatorade; I drank it without taking a breath.

In the van we took a winding tour of the area around the airfield. The area that was crossed by the Fifth was entirely overgrown. We came upon a Japanese tank with its treads blown off, exactly where it had died during the tank assault.

I found an empty napalm canister. It was made of thin aluminum, riveted. This one hadn't exploded. The jellied fuel must have leaked out.

North of the airfield we found the Japanese headquarters. It was an elaborate building, architecturally rendered; the staircase had a banister made of concrete. A bathroom featured a commode. The second floor was wide open. One wing of the building had massive steel doors; it was the room to which the officers would retreat during our naval bombardments. The doors hung open on their hinges. They had delayed the inevitable.

Tangie stayed in the van as I walked up a path leading into the hill facing the airfield. One large cave housed a 200-millimeter mortar. It was not on rails; it was anchored in the middle of a large gaping cave by steel supports that shot out like bristles, like sticks, to all four sides of the cave around it. It was suspended like a giant mother spider in a web. The barrel was wider than any gun barrel I'd ever imagined.

That evening I was back in my room, in the dark, when the rain started up and drummed against the roof of the guesthouse in a roar, then abated to a quiet drizzle. I couldn't sleep, so I went back out onto the street and dodged the puddles. I heard the sound of voices in song rising from an open door in the school—women practicing for the party. I poked my head in the doorway and smiled at the sound. They did not smile at me; I was not welcome there. It is deceptive, Palau's location, its virtual isolation from the rest of the planet; to stare off at its ocean horizons is to feel isolation of a magnitude I have never known, but clearly the social workings of the West were here: distrust, hostility, unease.

On the bench in front of the governor's office, in the light of a streetlight, sat a native. We exchanged greetings. He was enormously fat, and seemed to be friendly enough.

His eyes were bloodshot, but there was no scent of liquor on him. He was more pleasant than anyone I'd met here, and when he asked me to sit down, I quickly obliged. His name was Olsingch Ikar. I told him I was from New York. He told me he was in Los Angeles once, and he laughed.

"This is a well-tamed jungle," he said, with a wave at the darkness around us. "Los Angeles is a wild jungle."

By the lights outside of the governor's office, I could see the downpour patting the puddles. The surface of the water glowed a dull milky color from the coral and sandy mud.

Olsingch Ikar was in America in his teens, he told me. He returned to raise a family. He said he had three soldiers. I didn't understand; there is no army on Palau.

"Any time you have a boy," Olsingch explained, "he's gonna be a soldier. A policeman—something in a line of duty."

I asked him to tell me about the people of Peleliu.

"In Peleliu right now," he said, "the people are soft-spoken and close. Friendly people. Right now, people on Peleliu are just living the way they are supposed to be. No violence. They just want to maintain their place, their people, their family."

I thanked him for his time. I told him I intended to climb the hills to the north of the village the next morning.

"No bones up there," he told me. "They took all the bones."

Somewhere between the third day and the seventh day, the Fifth was pulled off the ridges in the south, circled back across the airfield and marched north to assault the hills from the west. Exactly when this happened is difficult for me to pin down; some of the men in the 1-5 remember assaulting the southern ridges in the first week, others the north. Most admit that, after they crossed the airfield, the entire battle becomes a blur—a series of endless and exhausting assaults on cave after cave after cave.

Unlike Guadalcanal, about which dozens of histories have been written in acute detail, Peleliu's story has been shrouded, from the first days when the marine correspondents were told by their editors that the real story in the South Pacific was MacArthur's return to the Philippines. MacArthur had, indeed, returned to the Philippines—unopposed. One week after the landing on Peleliu only five civilian correspondents remained on the island. Most of the dispatches that came to the states were written by marine correspondents.

I came across one of their dispatches in a file of records in the Corps's public affairs office in Manhattan. It read, in its entirety:

Jap Blows His Top on Palau

Peleliu, Palau Islands—The Japanese fighting man can be relied upon to provide the spectacular in suicide, but the enemy pulled a brand new one here, according to Technical Sergeant Benjamin Goldberg, a Marine Corps Combat Correspondent. One Jap, last of several snipers mopped up in the shell-ripped coconut grove, pulled the pin of a hand grenade, clapped it on his head and held his helmet over it.

It worked.

What is certain, I'd read in the official history, was that the Fifth marched up the western road, enduring heavy shelling from the hills to the right—"Hill Row," as it came to be called, a concentration of seven or eight low hills, arranged in a large L shape, in which the Japanese were concentrated in hundreds of caves. It was the Fifth's job to clear them out—specifically, a cave that I'd read had held more than 1,000 Japanese and featured a warren of eleven interlocking tunnels, constructed by a mining division. It had so many entrances and exits that the marines were never able to fully seal it up.

"There was that one mammoth cave," Don Peppard told me. "It commanded the path. The First Battalion tried to knock it out with machine-gun fire and grenades. Then the marines got on top of the cave and were slinging in thirty-five-pound satchel charges. That closed it. But the next day they were shooting out of it. So they got some amphibian tractors that had a snub-nosed 75 on them and fired in those, and that shut 'em up—and then the next day they were shooting out of there again. They finally got a 155 field piece and fired that point-blank in there. That closed it up for good."

The Fifth spent several days going into the hills and cleaning out the caves. By the end of the week the Fifth had eliminated 1,172 Japanese—most of them in cave-by-cave operations.

"The island was a catacomb of caves where they hewed that coral," Whiskey Williams said. "There was one underneath us one time—the fire was coming from underneath us. We called for a flamethrower. We throwed explosions into that hole. They throwed flamethrowers in, and here comes these Japs out. They tried to use a dead marine as a blind. I had a little guy with a water-jacket machine—no tripod—he had it in his hand. This Jap come out with his shirttail on fire and no shoes. My guy shot him down with the machine gun."

Herbert Ammons of the A-1-5 recalls amtracks with flamethrowers burning the Japanese out of their caves, and watching marines die on the hillside as friendly fire came in and hit them. Soldiers on stretchers, being administered plasma, tumbled down the steep ridge.

"The Japanese had been dug in all these many years," Ammons told me. "They had these holes that were like windows on the side of the mountains. The machine guns were set inside of the mountain."

Peleliu was not the first campaign in which the marines used flamethrowers, but it was the first campaign in which they used flamethrowers mounted on amtracks and tanks. The flamethrowers on Peleliu were high-powered and shot a stream of fuel four hundred yards like a laser line. A tape I saw not long ago, of newsreel footage of Peleliu, showed flame spitting from an American armored vehicle, and the line of fire was so precise that it looked like a video-game battle. This was the most effective weapon in the battle for Peleliu: flame directed at high speed, precisely, into a small opening from farther away than three football fields.

"They would throw flame a great distance and with considerable volume," Gordon Gayle told me. "You could squirt them out four hundred yards and keep it squirting and ignite it and let it burn. The same thing with napalm in gasoline tanks.

"We used a lot. But we should have used more."

Wasn't it savage? I asked him.

"You realize how savage it is. But hell—that worked both ways."

• • •

I left the village, walking north up the road, and climbed the first hill, the southernmost of Hill Row. Near the crest I found a large cave that disappeared into darkness; it appeared to have two levels. My flashlight illuminated a long tunnel. I walked back down, and continued north on the road. The ridge of hills to my right rose steeply and darkly. For several hundred yards the road went in a straight line north, the hills standing vigil above it. I walked on, hearing the crunch of my footsteps on the crushed coral. Fifty years earlier that road had been the bane of the Fifth Marines.

"They clobbered the hell out of the battalion," Rocco Zullo remembered. "We were facing this mountain, all these caves in it, and when they opened up with their artillery, it looked like the Fourth of July. Shells all over the place. The worst. Worse than the shelling on Guadalcanal. They just shelled the living hell out of us. We had several counterattacks we pushed back.

"We had nothing left," he said.

Zullo was knocked out at three in the morning one night when shrapnel dug a hole in his left shoulder "you could put a thumb in."

Bob Amery was hit in the same attack.

"Each unit in turn was getting slaughtered. The artillery opened up on us. As I was crawling toward a palm tree, a shell hit the tree. That was all I remember until I woke up on a hospital ship."

When Amery awoke, he was dismayed. Not because he was hurt. Because he was at sea.

"I'm squawking to my doctor, 'I gotta get back! I gotta

228

get back!' He said, 'What did you want to do? Win the war singlehanded?' "

A few hundred yards up the road, in the base of the northernmost hill, the central cave entrance yawns. The mouth is big enough to walk into, but it is pitch black. The hill that rises above it is too steep to ascend from the road, but I want to explore Hill Row, the scene of my father's last battles. The 1-5, according to *The Assault on Peleliu,* the marine corps's official account, was doing the bulk of the duty in the north; once these hills had been cleared out, the battle was effectively over.

I walked back down the road, looking for a way into the jungle, and finally I found one: a path perpendicular to the main road, between two hills. I walked for fifty yards or so, until I came across a large pit full of rusted fifty-gallon drums. Here I turned left and started to climb.

The hill soon turned steep; at times I had to pull myself up by tree roots, careful to find the ones that didn't pull right off; the coral was no more than six inches deep in the soil. Within a minute I had sweated through my clothes, and my hair was plastered to my head. The air felt as if it had been stuffed into the closed space beneath the canopy of trees.

The terrain turned steeper still, and a wall of bare coral loomed between me and the ridge above. At one point I was inching across its face on a twelve-inch ledge. Then the slope eased and I was atop the hill, walking on the ridge, a few yards wide. I came to a circle of coral wall, about six feet in diameter, about three feet high, which afforded a view to the north of more hills and, beyond them, the water.

• • •

"I was on outpost up there," Bob Shedd told me. "There was a round lookout made of coral. The company was down on the flat, and they used to send an outpost up there. I was in charge of the outpost one night when you could hear a Jap coming up. One of the guys shot at him, but he didn't hit him; in a little while you could hear him shuffling off. The third night we set up a thermite grenade so when it went off we'd be able to see him. But he never came.

"We had an awful lot of guys who were hurt up there," Bob Shedd told me. "Especially with grenades. Both sides were throwing them at night."

I sat on the coral wall to rest, listening to the birds call to each other in the treetops below me, watching the flight of a couple of brown sparrows colored like the dirt of the jungle floor, invisible until they moved. Suddenly I was startled by a splash of red: a bright red bird had lighted in a branch two feet from my face, certain for all of its life that there would be no people up here.

I stayed perfectly still. It was gone a moment later. In its place small green lizards skittered across the coral wall.

I plunged down the other side of the hill. It was as steep as the opposite slope I'd ascended. I lowered myself from branch to trunk to branch, my feet slipping in the loose, shifting soil. My arm brushed a branch, and when ants spilled out, I had anticipated them; my reflexes were getting better. I swatted them away before a single ant could sting me.

As the slope grew more gradual, I found myself in a

clearing of huge flat stones. Some rose out of the ground at odd angles; others looked as if they'd been dropped on top of the first ones—they looked as randomly dropped as the stones by the side of a mountain creek, except that some were twenty and thirty and forty feet across. The spaces beneath them, and in between them, would not be called caves in the strict sense of the word, but they were wide enough for a man to get in and out. Each featured one or two spots of darkness, like empty eye sockets.

A slice of darkness two feet wide represented the mouth to one of the caves; on top of it was a large boulder, twenty feet across and six or eight feet thick, seemingly suspended in the air; its other half was buried in the hillside. Its mouth commanded a view of the valley, which was several dozen yards wide, and then, across it, the side of another hill. This cave would hold a dozen men. Maybe far more.

I got on my belly and crawled in, with my flashlight ahead of me. A moment later I was no longer crawling on the dirt, but across what I immediately knew to be an ancient garbage pit, full of empty rusted cans and large glass bottles. I pulled out a bottle and slithered backward into the light. I held a brown quart beer bottle. Raised Japanese characters broke the surface of the glass. I crawled back into the cave and rummaged around. My hands found untold empty beer bottles: The Japanese had crawled into this cave, got drunk, and died.

I walked farther down the slope until it leveled into the narrow valley. I decided against climbing the opposite slope, and turned to walk down the valley, toward where I figured the road would be. But a half-hour later, after I'd stopped to poke my head into a few more caves, I'd still found no road, and the grass grew taller than I; before long I tangled in grass and vines much stronger than I:

determined to plow through, I found myself completely wrapped up in vines and grass, trying to beat them away, trying to untangle myself.

To the objective observer I would have looked like a madman, swatting at inanimate vines, panicked. At one point, trying to forge my way through the thicket toward the open horizon I glimpsed at the end of the valley, I became so ensnarled that I could not even turn around. I had to walk backward several yards until, finally free, I turned around and realized that, while I was fairly certain of the direction I'd been walking from, I had no idea how long I'd been walking: it could have been ten minutes; it could have been an hour. I had no idea where the caves were up on the hillside that would serve as my navigational guide back the way I came.

I worked my way back down the valley, trying to peer up through the trees to find the caves. Finally, fearing that I'd missed them, I struck up the hillside anyway. If I had missed them and gone past them, it occurred to me that I would climb the hill and come down on the other side in the jungle somewhere northeast of the village.

In fact, I had done a very foolish thing. I had told no one what I was going to do or where I was going. Then, I didn't imagine they'd have cared a great deal. I couldn't envision the villagers of Peleliu sending out a search party for me.

I climbed, and climbed farther, churning through the leaves and earth, scraping my knuckles on coral, until I was on the ridge again. I followed it eastward for a few minutes, and saw the coral lookout. I did not stop to rest this time, but descended quickly, in what I hoped would be a straight line. When I reached the bottom of the hill, the oil drums were nowhere to be seen. It took another ten minutes of zigzagging through the jungle, trying to suppress the instinct to shout for help, until I saw one drum, then another, then finally the pit. Next to the pit was the path out.

I walked down the path to the road, and headed back to the village, huffing. In retrospect, it seems fitting that I was rescued by rusted wreckage. At the time it didn't cross my mind.

I had had my fill of all of it now.

I know where my father was in the final two weeks. *The Assault on Peleliu* was explicit. I'd been somewhat stunned to find in its campaign maps dated the first two weeks of October—the third and fourth weeks of the campaign—that the north of the island was designated by something called the Richmond Group. It was a detachment of the Pioneer Battalion, the battalion used to organize the shore party. The Pioneers' duty was to get people onto and off the island. By definition, the Pioneers were not a combat battalion, but on Peleliu everyone was a combat soldier. My father had been put in command of a group of Pioneers whose job was to anchor the north if the Japanese, flushed out by the marines to the south, fled to the north.

Gordon Gayle told me, "That would have been someone saying, 'We want a good solid citizen up there. Here's old Tom Richmond.' "

By late October it was time for the Fifth Regiment to be relieved. They had lived up to the billing: they'd been the first ashore and the last to leave. In the final reckoning the Fifth Marine Regiment accounted for 70 percent of the First Marine Division's objectives. The casualty rate was about the same. The casualty rate among the machine-gun squads was 82 percent. As Bob Amery recalls it, "Battalions were down to a platoon. Companies were down to squads."

On October 27 my father left the work of the Richmond Group to someone else. He went down to Orange Beach One, boarded a launch, and was taken to sea, beyond the reef, where he boarded the SS *Sea Runner.* Four days later he arrived at Pavuvu. His war was over.

According to his records, he was the battalion commander again for ten days on Pavuvu, no doubt while Boyd was sent home, and the battalion awaited the arrival of the next colonel. I do know that in his five weeks on Pavuvu my father ate well.

"We'd buried a case of wine in the corner of our tent," H. L. Opie told me. "We were assigned to the same tent [they'd occupied before the invasion of Peleliu]. You could get meat and eggs and things. With a little bit of wine, you could get about anything you wanted."

According to Bill Looney, my father made certain that the 1-5 was well provided for on Thanksgiving, when their own rations did not arrive. He led a raid on a neighboring outfit.

"They took a Jeep over and stole half of their turkeys and had a jolly time," Looney told me. "He didn't feel too bad about it. He needed his people to have a Thanksgiving dinner."

On November 25, Colonel Kunio Nakagawa radioed, "All is over on Peleliu," and disemboweled himself with a jeweled dagger.

In 1947 the last Japanese soldier was coerced out of the big cave. A Japanese prisoner of war, an admiral, was brought over from Guam to coerce him out with a loud-speaker.

At the south end of the island, the Seabees built a huge B-29 base, and dockage for carriers and battleships. None ever came. No planes. No ships. Peleliu had served no strategic purpose whatsoever.

"The whole damn thing was unnecessary," Don Peppard told me. "There was no necessity. No reason in the world that magnificent division should have gone in there. We had neutralized their airpower. That stinking dinky little airport couldn't support anything of a major threat to MacArthur. Rupertus told the troops that we would sweep them clean out of there in four to five days? For God's sake —they were still there two years later! He didn't know what the hell was going on. What could you do once you landed? There was no great enfilading movement you could do. There was nothing you could do but go right straight at them. Right at the cliffs. But nothing worked. They sent tanks up there, flamethrowers, we bombed it— nothing worked. You were just firing at these positions they'd prepared for twenty years! But they'd been neutral-ized! It just wasn't worth sacrificing everybody. Or any-body.

"Not those kids," Don Peppard said. "Not those young marines."

"We had no damned business being there," Ray Fenton told me. "Let alone being killed."

The most poignant legacy of Peleliu, and one of the strongest symbols of the abomination of the campaign, was the utter failure of the man who was the marines' highest-profile leatherneck. Chesty Puller's First Regiment was annihilated. Puller's men were slaughtered in the coral ridges inland from the beach. In the first week Puller's regiment had suffered 1,672 casualties. He'd keep throwing his men at the ridges, and they'd keep dying—as he had thrown my father and his men across the Matanikau, with no hope of their getting across.

On the seventh day of the campaign Major General Geiger visited Puller at his command post and relieved the famed soldier, over Rupertus's objections.

Don Peppard remembers that day, remembers the surprising moment when he was alone in regiment headquarters on the north of the island and Major General Geiger showed up from his ship, the *Mount McKinley,* three thousand yards offshore.

"I was sitting up at our command post up on the northwest end of the island," Peppard told me. "I was the only one there. In came Major General Geiger. I told him everything I could. He sat down on a coconut log. Then he said, 'I'm never going to let an operation get away from me like this one.' "

In his evaluation of my father at the end of October 1944, Colonel Boyd gave my father ten "excellents" and one "outstanding." The "outstanding" was in "loyalty." Boyd checked the space for "particularly desire to have him."

In the "Remarks" section, Boyd wrote simply, "Levelheaded and courageous in action."

Maybe Boyd wasn't a wordy man. Maybe he was busy fighting the battle. Maybe all he said said it all.

• • •

By the time I reached the main road, I was so thirsty I could think of nothing but drinking. I walked back through the village, toward a store I had seen south of the town. I approached a gazebo built in front of a house, in which a half-dozen teenaged boys played a game of pool. They were laughing and listening to music on a boom box. As I walked by, they stopped talking and stared at me until I was out of earshot. On my walk back, again the boys fell silent. Emboldened by my exhaustion, I said hello. None of them answered.

I had grown tired of such treatment, and angry. So I sat down on the bench in front of the governor's office and opened my notebook and waited. I had climbed my last hill. I had lost my taste for it. I could not stop thinking about the cave—the slit, really—into which I'd crawled. There had been no more than two feet of space beneath the boulder, but it had been deep enough for a dozen men to die there.

The front door of a house down the street opened up, and a man came out and walked directly toward me. He sat down on the bench and introduced himself. His name was Ichick Idesiar. He was smiling. He told me he was fifty-six. We spent several minutes making small talk. Then his expression changed.

"The American federals come here to build monuments, but they don't give you something to help the government," he said. "They come back on anniversary? Big ceremony. They left the next day."

I believe he thought I would listen to him and write down what he said and take his message back to the American government. He told me that what he was saying now he had told the American officials. I assumed he meant the American officials who dedicated the small monument in the village in 1985, and the soldiers who had come the month before me.

"Let me tell you the truth," he said. "Peleliu was one of the richest islands in all of Palau. During the Japanese time here, my father said, you plant five, six papaya, four banana. But now, only coconut grows. We are very poor now. Banana? Papaya? No more. The Second World War washed away the soil. And the fish gone, too. Maybe the bomb poison the reefs. Kill the natural things under the water."

The two-day preinvasion bombardment had included 519 rounds of 16-inch shells; 1,845 rounds from the 14-inch guns; 1,793 500-pound bombs and 73,412 .50-caliber machine-gun bullets. According to John Costello's *Pacific War,* by the time the battle was over, it had taken 1,589 rounds of light and heavy ammunition to kill each enemy soldier.

"Last year the DEA came," Mr. Idesiar told me. He shook his head in disgust. "Three years ago the crop was four and a half million dollars. Two and a half years ago, three million. Now this month, one and a half. Last time, they don't burn. They bring to Koror."

Marijuana?

"We plant and sell," he told me. "Only the tops—not the young ones. That is Peleliu economy. That is what pays. The DEA man, his name is James, he says, 'Oh, yes, I understand, but this is illegal.' I say, 'But this is illegal for America.' You, you Americans, you use your policy to stop marijuana. This is economic. This is business. This is our economy."

He waved toward his house across the street.

"That house is marijuana house. Marijuana pays. We have car, pickup truck. That is marijuana money. A house! My house, very hard to buy if I selling fish. You see this car passing? That's the money from marijuana. Go to Babelthuap. You cannot see cars! Motorbikes!"

I was writing—a little furiously, I suppose; the journalist in me had kicked in. I couldn't help but see the curiosity of it: two thousand of the finest American soldiers had lost their lives so that a twelve-square-mile coral atoll could grow, half a century later, the most potent marijuana on the planet.

And then I noticed a man sitting on the other side of Ichick, several yards away: the same wild-eyed, wild-haired guy who had observed my conversation with the Peace Corps worker. He appeared to be wearing the same clothes he'd been wearing two days earlier. He was definitely wearing the same half-smile. He looked as if he were out of his mind.

I conspicuously leaned forward to see past Ichick and stare down at the man. He stared back at me without changing his expression.

I rose, and hoped Ichick would go with me as I walked down the road. He did. He led me through his backyard, and another, until suddenly we stood before a large blasted-out two-story concrete bunker. It was the radio station that Rocco Zullo's company took out on the twenty-eighth of September, 1944.

We climbed up the wide stairway to the second floor. I walked to the edge and looked down at the backyards of the houses on the road.

I asked Ichick about his customers. Americans, Japanese, Taiwanese, Koreans, he told me. Especially Japanese.

Japanese tourism is a large part of Palau's income. Ichick was proud of the quality of Peleliu's crop.

"It is very good," he told me. "It is what we call 'trip.' The DEA man say they test in laboratory—ours the best. He say that it's better than Philippines, Guam, Taiwan, Hong Kong, Mexico, Thailand. He say, 'We don't know how you do it. How you fertilize?' "

He smiled with pride.

"I said to the DEA man, 'Maybe you smoke?' He said, 'Oh, my friend, I know what you say, but this is my job.' I said, 'Let us sell. I give you fresh natural coconut.' He say, 'Ah, not this time.' "

I asked him how people got the marijuana through customs. He told me that one Japanese man told him they pay off the postmaster and the customs officials back home, and then mail it, and then telephone home for a special message to see if it got through.

I was surprised at his frankness; it was possible that he never quite understood I wasn't an emissary from the government. The journalist in me was grateful; the paranoid in me could not stop seeing the man in the fatigue jacket. As I thanked Ichick for his time and wished him the best, I couldn't help wondering whether I could anticipate that evening, in the guest house, in the middle of the night, a visit from the man with the wild hair and some of his wild friends. Perhaps if only to confiscate my notebook. Perhaps something more severe.

I was due to fly out the following day and catch a connecting flight to Manila. I had hoped to see the party at the school that evening, to watch them celebrate, in the hopes that someone would trust me and share some insight about the place and its history and its war. No one had invited me, though, and if I attended, I'd probably just force them to smoke their pot furtively instead of in the open.

I found Tangie mowing his lawn with a modern gasoline-powered lawn mower. Was it too late to get today's plane? No, he told me, not if we hurried.

I stuffed my clothes and souvenirs into my bags. He took me to the airport, smiling and giggling at something I didn't understand. He made me promise to send pictures of my father for his museum. As the van reached the airstrip, the Paradise Air plane was taxiing in. The door opened and two white people jumped out. They looked like the kind of people I used to meet in interstate highway culverts in the days when I used to hitchhike across the States. They introduced themselves to me—Rolf and Josephine. They were Austrian. Josephine was in her early twenties—pretty, and much too thin. Rolf appeared to be a few years older. He had long blond dreadlocks that did not appear to have ever been washed. His teeth were rotting. He told me they heard it was a great island. He wanted to know if they could sleep on the beach. They appeared to be high already—members of a quiet subset of society that apparently searches the globe for the best drugs that nature can provide. I can only assume they found what they were looking for.

I thanked Tangie for his help and climbed into the plane. A large kid from Peleliu wearing shades and a gold watch and a camouflage-patterned jacket with U.S. MARINE written above the breast pocket climbed in next to me. He nodded at me. I nodded back. The true paranoid in me thought for a moment that he had been sent to follow me to Koror, where he would confiscate my notebook and stuff me into a trash can.

241

My flight back to Manila, to transfer to Los Angeles, left Koror at dawn. I was first in line to go through customs. The agent opened all of my bags.

After the two-hour flight to Manila, I waited in the international departures lounge for twelve hours, then boarded the flight home. It was Saturday night when I arrived in Los Angeles. I was carrying a lot of bags. I was unwashed, ragged, and giddy. I told the immigration officer where I'd been. He looked at my visa stamps, and then looked at something on his computer. He nodded and passed me through his line, whereupon I was immediately pulled aside by another official, who took me to a special line. There was no one in the line except me. I had set off various warning signs, apparently; I had fit a profile.

He asked me to open everything. He took a wooden carved Palau storyboard and examined it inch by inch for secret seams and hiding compartments. He was certain he had detained a smuggler of illegal narcotics. I did not want to open anything. I wanted to get home.

I unzipped one bag and pulled out the official marine monograph about the battle of New Britain. It was dog-eared and the spine was crumbling. I told my tale as I'd told it many times before. I opened the book and thrust it at him.

He looked at the black and white photographs of marines wading through swamps. He started turning the pages. He forgot about searching for drugs.

"I heard in some of those battles," he said as he handed the book back to me, "the alligators were big enough to eat the soldiers."

"On New Britain," I told him, "there were pythons nine feet long."

He zipped up my bags and welcomed me home.

I arrived home on a Sunday afternoon. Monday's mail—literally, the next day—included a thick envelope from the Awards Division of the Personnel and Records people in St. Louis. They'd finally gotten around to sending me my father's awards records. Anxiously I opened the envelope, expecting to read that he'd won the Bronze Star on some battlefield I'd missed.

The first thing I noticed, along with a sheaf of papers, was a leather box stamped SILVER STAR MEDAL in gold lettering. I assumed they'd sent a copy of my father's Silver Star. I'm conditioned to think that things are readily copied. I didn't stop to think that, to the marines, a Silver Star is a somewhat sacred thing; no one would devalue it by duplicating it.

There were several pieces of paper included in the packet. The first one was a cover letter, dated 1951. It read:

The recommendation originally submitted in Lieutenant Colonel Richmond's case was reviewed by the Navy Department Board of Decorations and Medals, which Board recommended that the Bronze Star Medal previously awarded him for his service on Peleliu Island, Palau Group, from 15 to 29 September 1944, be recalled and canceled, and that, in lieu thereof, he be awarded a Gold Star in lieu of a second Silver Star Medal. It is also requested that the Bronze

Star medal with permanent citation be secured before the Gold Star in lieu of a Second Silver Star Medal and citation are presented.

He had won a second Silver Star. I opened the black leather oblong box with the gold legend SILVER STAR MEDAL embossed on it. When I opened the box, a puff of dusty scent greeted my nostrils. This box hadn't been opened since 1951. Apparently they'd kept it, waiting for my father to return his Bronze Star, and now, forty-three years later, they'd decided what the hell, and just sent me the medal.

Unlike the first Silver Star, which was tarnished and dull, handled a great many times in the last half-century before it had finally reached me, this one was perfect and brilliant —I'd grown so accustomed to looking at the first one that I had difficulty recognizing this one as the same medal: a bright gold star, a silver star in the middle of it. The ribbons were so red, white, and blue they were almost garish. The medal was nestled on pumpkin-colored velvet. The inside of the top of the box was fashioned of padded satin of the same color.

The accompanying citation said, "Exposing himself almost constantly to hostile machine-gun and rifle fire, Major Richmond led a combat patrol of two companies (reinforced) with skill, aggressiveness and determination against a numerically superior enemy in well-fortified mutually supporting caves."

In the Marine Corps Historical Center I found a book that lists all of the medal award winners in the Marine Corps from 1861 to 1955. It is called *Heroes*. It explained that any time a marine is awarded a second Silver Star, it is a Gold Star.

According to this book, 3,916 marines—of a fighting force of more than 400,000—received Silver Stars in the Second World War.

Seventy-four won two of them.

The mutually supporting caves, whose cross fire he braved, might well have flanked the very valley in which I had been lost. I may have crawled into one of the caves whose annihilation he had ordered.

It would only stand to reason that my father would know where to find the cave with the beer.

Retired Brigadier General Gordon Gayle's room in the Riviera Hotel in Las Vegas is on the sixteenth floor. Below us, out the window, the pool is clotted with sunbaked Americans; at five o'clock the sun feels like a noontime sun.

Gayle has brought out a flask of scotch. I have chopped up a block of ice in his sink. He is drinking Perrier and Famous Grouse on the rocks. I have skipped the Perrier.

Gordon Gayle has been asked by the Marine Corps Historical Society to write a fiftieth-anniversary history of the battle of Peleliu. His monograph is overdue. He has been trying to find the right way to write it.

"I have to figure out a way to tell the truth," he tells me, "and still be able to say to the commandant of the marine corps, 'This is an appropriate thing for you to publish.' "

Gayle had the 2-5 on Peleliu, where he was awarded the Navy Cross as battalion commander for getting his battalion across the airfield first. He is as solid an example of the Marine Corps's efficiency, prowess, and intelligence

as you could ever hope to find. But at the Las Vegas reunion, his time is spent dragging the marine command
across the coals. I have found him in conversation at various times down in the ballroom with various veterans, and
each conversation has concerned itself with the flaws in
the strategy, the tragedy of the tactics, and the useless bravery of the men. Fifty years after his graduation from the
United States Naval Academy, the strain of having to ex-
pose the corps's shortcomings is obvious. We spend an
hour discussing all manner of things military—for me it's
like having an intense seminar at the Naval Academy. I am
making up for a lifetime of ignorance of the military, and I
know that in this moment, over good scotch, in the company of a clearly eloquent man, I have a chance to make
up some ground. Gayle speaks to me of Hannibal, and
General Washington, and battlefield strategy. He tells me
of the German Naval League, and of the strategies for
assaulting a medieval castle, and of the backbone that
Lejeune instilled in the Corps in the thirties.

But every few minutes, the talk returns to Peleliu. Gordon Gayle knows as well as anyone that the Corps would
have gladly accepted a cursory piece of work in his fiftieth-
anniversary retrospective book. He also knows he was unable to deliver one. I suspect that the rigor he's brought to
the project is his payback to the men of his battalion sent
to a needless death fifty years ago.

"It should not have been fought, as the Philippines campaign should not have been fought," he tells me.

"We didn't need to go to the Philippines at all. In the
summer of 'forty-four, Nimitz said, 'We have the where-
withal to go right straight across the Pacific.' MacArthur
said, 'You've got to return to the Philippines. I made a
promise.'

"[And] given that the Philippines campaign had to be fought, Peleliu still need not have been fought. The big argument is whether Peleliu was necessary. In hindsight, it wasn't. Halsey knew it on Friday before the game—[and] everybody else knows it on Monday. The real question is, 'Why the hell [did] we go to the Philippines at all, other than MacArthur's ego?' That's why we went. The only rational explanation of it was that Nimitz made the commitment to support MacArthur at that July conference, and Nimitz's agreement to not take Palau could have been interpreted as a default to that commitment. Nobody knows."

I apologize in advance for the next question: How, now, does he feel about Peleliu?

"I feel terrible about it," he says. "This is the one thing that it's been hard for me to come to grips with: the fact that I lost sixty percent of my officers and fifty percent of my men to a campaign that did not need to be fought."

Before I leave his room, I ask Gordon Gayle why, after four years at the Naval Academy, he decided to join the marines and not the Navy—the fashionable branch of the armed services. He says something about not particularly liking ships, and about being impressed with the marine officers he met while he was at the Academy.

Then he says: "There wasn't a difficult choice. I never met a sailor who admitted he was proud to be a sailor. I never met a marine who said he wasn't proud to be a marine."

On the elevator ride down to the lobby, I ask Gordon Gayle about my father.

"Tom was a very modest guy, competent and brave. Tom wouldn't come back and beat his chest and say he was brave. He just was. That's all."

. . .

I glance around the ballroom, at the dozens of men staring into their beers, and part of me is glad that he is not here. I know that if he'd lived he'd have been here, and I don't think I'd want to know he'd be at one of these tables, with the bad memories flitting at the corners of his eyes.

His men told me he'd never miss a reunion. He'd reserve tables for his enlisted men, so they could be near the action. Several recalled that the last they saw of him was at a reunion. But I give a silent prayer of thanks that I never saw him folded in on himself, feeling bad that he'd survived. I am glad to be able to imagine him only as the compact, muscular young captain darting up and down Edson's Ridge, filling gaps, shouting orders; as the underaged major wading up the muck of the creek on Natamo Point; as the jaded veteran snaking his platoon into the valleys of Hill Row on Peleliu.

Heroism is not what I thought it was. Seen from the point of view of the men who fought the war, what I thought of as heroism turned out to be nothing more than doing one's job. Here, in the Riviera ballroom, I am learning the nature of what my father really was, and here, among a thousand like him, my quest is coming to an end.

I am relinquishing my father the ideal, and coming to terms with my father the man, and allowing myself, finally —much later than most of the people I know—to let go of him.

The men who have gathered here fought because they thought they had no choice, and, probably, they didn't. To have shirked the call would have been heresy. So they climbed into amtracks, and sang their nervous songs to keep each other's spirits up as the beach grew closer, and piled out with their friends, and watched their friends die at their sides, and pushed on until they couldn't push any more on a chunk of sharp and barren coral on the absolute other side of the planet, because everyone else was doing it, and they'd never have been able to live with themselves if they hadn't.

Fifty years later we wonder at what they did, at their selflessness, but the truth of it—I knew now, two years after the day I pulled Harry Connor's letters out of a cardboard box in Washington—is that, if we had to, we'd do the same thing. Forced to die for our friends—for people who would instinctively die for us, people like Carlton Rouh—we probably would. Now I think I would. The point is not that people change, because they don't. Circumstances do. I no longer need worry about whether I could have been him. I could have.

If anything has changed, it's that we no longer have anyone forcing us to be anything; no overarching moral imperative rules in a land grown complacent, grown so secure that its last three presidents have picked petty wars over petty issues, seemingly just to have a war. We've gained more freedom as individuals—and, judging from the chaos and confusion underlying end-of-the-millennium America, lost it all back as a society, fallen into a balancing bankruptcy on the other side of the ledger.

None of my father's men would tell you they fought for an ideal; they'll tell you they fought for each other. On a basic level, heroism is nothing more than the willingness to sacrifice your life for something you believe in. My father's men believed in a couple of things. First and foremost, you had to be willing to die to defend your friends, because your friends would do the same for you, a credo derived from the respect every man had for the lives that surrounded him. Most of the men in Las Vegas had friends die for them. It wasn't just the honorable thing to do; it was the only thing to do.

The respect my father had for his men was apparent at every corner, from the enlisted men who'd visited him at the farm, to the half-dozen who told me he'd had them out for dinner at his folks' house in Yonkers, to the enlisted man at whose court-martial proceedings he testified. But I knew now that, in so doing, he was not acting unusually. "One thing we had was respect for the enlisted men," John Jachym, another officer in the 1-5, told me. "I still get visits, calls, letters from all my platoons. I was closer to the men in my rifle platoon than I ever was again to any other group of men."

Jachym told me the story of the day when his sergeant showed up on his doorstep for a visit, years after the war, and gave his name, and started to introduce himself to Jachym's wife.

"I know who you are," John Jachym's wife said, and opened the door wide.

The second thing they were willing to sacrifice for, to preserve with that sacrifice, was America. Perhaps right now we don't feel as if we have anything all that worth preserving. It's been five decades since we had a war we believed in, and in those five decades we've not only lost any idea about what it is to fight a good war, we've lost any understanding about having to sacrifice young men's lives to protect the common good.

In the Second World War the cause was nothing less

than the American way of life, which had proven itself over the previous century to be, if not perfect, at the very least a workable democracy. We must have thought it was worth saving. "We know what we have to face and we know we are ready to face it," Eleanor Roosevelt said in her radio broadcast for NBC the night of December 7. "Whatever is asked of us, I am sure we can accomplish it; we are the free and unconquerable people of the U.S.A."

If you're paying for your way of life with young men's lives, then logic dictates that that way of life must be something special, and you treat it with some respect. But if now, for the first time in the history of the nation, no one has to die to preserve that way of life, isn't it inevitable that we'd come to lose some respect for it?

Not many of my father's men cited defending the American way of life as a driving force, although some did. Leonard Lawton was one who had.

"Well, you know, we all were gung-ho patriots," Leonard Lawton told me. "That sounds weird, I know. But we were ready to do anything for America and we were proud to be American marines. We wanted to go, too. We had to go, but we didn't resist it. We knew that this was something that had to be done. We were ready. And when it was over, we didn't expect any ticker tape parade. We were just boys coming home."

On the other hand, Leonard Lawton was also the first to point out to me that he'd only enlisted in the marines because he didn't want to be drafted. Better to have some say in your future than none. "I did not want to be known as a draftee," Lawton told me.

Many of my father's soldiers had similar tales: "I didn't

251

want to be drafted, I wanted to pick my own destiny," John Jachym told me. "To me, the French Foreign Legion and the marines were the best."

Few had been drawn in by the need to go off and kill, or to get killed. They were lured by decidedly mundane temptations. One had been laid off his job as a construction worker at the Choate School in Wallingford, Connecticut—which I would attend thirty years later. Another had failed to get into law school, as my father's low natural-science grades at Dartmouth had kept him out of medical school.

They were a generation of men who were facing a Depression job market. Some, like my father, would have done anything rather than go into the family business. One didn't want to be a farmer, like his father. Another had had it at a small-town newspaper; one day an application to the marine ROTC caught his eye.

"My first indoctrination to the Marine Corps was a cigarette ad in a magazine," Richard Nellson told me. "This man and this woman were sitting on a patio in the advertisement, looking over this harbor, and here's this great big white cruiser in the bay. And the guy's in his whites, and I looked at that and I thought, 'Oh, Geez, that's for me.'

"And after I got into a few tight places," he said, "I said to myself, 'You made sort of a poor judgment there.' "

Was he a hero?

"I think I never have gone whole-hog on the fact that I saved the world or saved the United States," Nellson told me. "I just figured it was something that had to be done, and that you got into it and you wanted to see it through."

"I thought the marines were associated with ships and the sea," Frank Bacon told me. "I thought that would be a much nicer organization, to my liking. I knew that they didn't take just anybody—they were pretty selective. And I was interested in associating myself with people who I felt were worthy of getting to know well."

"When you have a platoon or a company, you're responsible for people, you don't have time to think, you got your job to do and you do it," Maurice Raphael said. "That's not being heroic. That's what they hired you for. All I knew was you wore blue uniforms and supposedly did a lot of embassy duty. I didn't know about the GDFMF."

The what?

"The Goddamned Fleet Marine Force," he said, laughing. "But things were very different then. We didn't have any better sense. We thought that was the heroic thing. We were all too dumb to know any better."

A legion of them insisted that they'd enlisted for no great reason, that they had no overarching desire to save mankind. The fact remains that once they were faced with having to do so, they did.

Bob Amery enlisted in Boston in 1940 because there were no jobs to be had—"and I liked that Marine Corps blue uniform. I thought it sounded pretty good. They gave me a song and dance about how you can get an education in there with the Marine Corps Institute, which turned out to be nothing but a correspondence school."

But whatever Amery's original inclination, once he wore the uniform, he became a man answering to a fairly high call. Signing up for the snappy uniforms is one thing. It's another to land in an amtrack on Peleliu when each amtrack on either side of you is being blown out of the water; to cross an airfield while hearing bullets hit your buddies;

to take a machine gun out of an amtrack splattered by a man's insides, and get hit by shrapnel yourself—and to wake up seven days later on a hospital boat and tell the doctor you have to get back, you've got to return to the most hellish twelve square miles anyone had ever known.

"Well, you felt that you had to," Bob Amery told me. "Nothing else occurred to you. It was your duty. This was your job. You were expected to do that. There wasn't any choice."

I found Amery in the A-1-5 hospitality suite, with Russ Clay and Lou Schott and Birddog Clayton, up on the twenty-sixth floor of the Riviera. Lou Schott is much smaller than I thought he'd be, since I knew he'd tackled Irvin Cleveland on the other side of the airstrip, but his handshake is a strong grip, and his eyes are kind and gentle. I recognize him from the photograph of the volleyball team on Pavuvu, squinting into the sun.

Amery turns out to have snow-white hair, but he looks about twenty years younger than I thought he would. He's drinking a beer. At the bar in the suite on the twenty-sixth floor, Birddog Clayton is mixing a mai tai for Bob's wife. Out the window the white light of desert sun beats against the city; the cigarette smoke in the suite makes it hard to see out the window.

Across the coffee table sits Larry Kerwin of the A-1-5. He'd stowed away to land on Peleliu, he tells me. Russ Clay is sitting with his back to the picture window, ignoring the view of the city and the desert. In the chair next to him, a Korean War vet slugs his beer. He is the only man who has let the drink get the better of him on this afternoon. He is bemoaning the fact that none of his Korea buddies made it to the reunion. He is blinking back the beer and nodding at the half-dozen silver-haired warriors in the loud shirts and polyester baseball caps with the bellies like bowling balls, scattered around the room, not laughing, but smiling.

"These guys are my heroes," he says again and again. "These guys are my heroes."

Rocco Zullo grew up in a lumber camp in New Hampshire, he tells me at the C-1-5 table. In front of him is a photograph of the battalion taken before Guadalcanal. When Rocco told his father he wanted to enlist, his father refused to sign him up, so Rocco rode the freights west to Denver and enlisted out there. He had his sister fake his father's signature and sent the letter out West. It worked.

I meet Rocco in person when a man from the C-1-5 named Jerry McHale comes over and says, "Was your father Curly Tom Richmond?"

I allow as how he probably was.

"Rocco says he knew your dad," McHale says, and nods at a man at another table wearing a red, white, and blue First Marine Division cap. Rocco is sitting with some C-1-5 men. Tom (The Greek) Panouses, Hank Paustian. Rocco sits me down and tells the table I'm Curly Tom's son.

When I ask Rocco about the time he took the radio center on Peleliu, he tells me that Jack the Mack—now Retired Lieutenant General John McLaughlin—had recommended him for the Navy Cross for that operation. The paperwork got lost.

When I start to write the tale down, Rocco reaches out a beefy hand and places it on my arm.

"Aw, don't put that in there," Rocco says. "I'm alive. I'm in one piece. That's all I wanted. I finally ended up marrying a Navy nurse. I never would have married my Navy nurse if I hadn't been wounded. I had six children.

"So you see why I don't want anything?"

I don't understand.

"Why I don't want any awards. Any medals. See, everything turned out for the best."

There's something else about your father being a war hero, of course, which is that if he really was, the son is living with a formidable example to follow. I had never considered the possibility that I was trying to live up to his standard—and, like most sons, failing—because, unlike other fathers of other sons, mine wasn't around for me to emulate or disappoint. How could I be trying to live up to standards I hadn't even known about?

In truth, the fact that he wasn't around for me to see his failures and flaws might have made him an even more difficult role model. But I have now seen him through the eyes of those who knew him in the war, and I have come to realize that he was not so much an extraordinary man as a good man—one among many—in extraordinary times. And now that I know this, maybe now I can go on with my life.

I have discovered that he was no superman—at least, not by the standards of mid-century America. But that does not mean that we shouldn't think of these men, for what they did, as men of honor. They understood sacrifice, and that is no small thing. We've always had war and we've always known about the necessity for sacrifice. Soldiers and heretics and explorers and all great men have always assumed that death in pursuit of their goals was a likely possibility. It's no longer true. It is a tragic loss.

One morning during the convention, the marines line up outside the hotel behind the Marine Corps band from Camp Pendleton. The setting strikes me as ignominious: they will march into the back lobby of the hotel by coming up a driveway jammed in between the pink stucco wall of the ballroom and the pink cement parking garage.

The band is so sharp that every note blasts from the brass like a tangible thing. It is a march, and in this unusual locale, the music is amplified as the sound bounces from the stucco to the cement; they are playing in an open tunnel, and it is so crisp, so loud, that a thousand old marines, bent by age, slackened by time and grief, start to straighten up. Now they are marching in place. They are champing to get going, even if their objective is nothing but a set of AstroTurfed stairs into an air-conditioned Las Vegas ballroom. Even if no one is watching them but family, and parking attendants, and gawking tourists who wonder what in the world they've stumbled into, this bizarre setting has, instead of diminishing their dignity, served to magnify it.

The C-1-5 is at the head of the parade. Someone is carrying a C-1-5 flag. Suddenly, Rocco Zullo steps from the crowd, and takes his place to the right of the column, and now he's chanting "Harch! Harch! Harch!" and they are in step. They are all in step. Zullo is shouting over the band, you can hear it all over the city, and the look on his face is a look that I will never forget. It is the look that I never got to see my father wear—until now, on Rocco Zullo's face.

They march past, up the stairs, into the lobby, toward the ballroom. And in the lobby, a couple of dozen tourists suddenly break into applause, and the applause starts to grow, it ripples down the carpeted hallways toward the casino, and they file past, still in step, ducking their flags so as not to poke the ceiling, eyes fixed straight ahead.

On the last morning of the convention the G-2-5 holds a reunion of its own. George Hadzidakis is there. The years have been good to George Hadzidakis. The lenses of his glasses are thick, but his wit is all there. He remembers a night my father recited "Dangerous Dan McGrew." They are, all of them, mining their memories for slices of Tom Richmond, knowing that anything at all is all that I want. George is wearing a bolo tie clip with the word GUADALCA-NAL embedded in it in silver. Jack Parrish and Theron Cordray are there, too, chain-smoking their Pall Malls.

Art Beres is there. My father ordered Art Beres across the Matanikau. Beres lost his entire squad before he himself was evacuated by a corpsman. When I first see Art, it is from the left side, and his profile is normal. When he turns to face me, I see that the right side of his face has never recovered. It balloons out. Its features have been rearranged. It is a maze of skin grafts.

"I reached up after I got shot and realized my whole jawbone was sticking out," he tells me. "Eventually they grafted part of my hip into my jaw."

Then Elmer Miller comes into the room and asks if he can see me alone for a moment. I excuse myself from the table and stand up. I figure I know what it's about. I figure that Elmer Miller has had a couple of nights to think about what he'd told me about his tears, and his dead buddies, and his inability to cope with Peleliu's horrors—and thought better of it. He was the only marine I knew who had been forthcoming about the war getting to him, and getting the better of him. I figure he wants to tell me that what he'd said the other day was off the record.

Instead he leads me over to another table, where there's a scrapbook, open to a page with a small, faded snapshot of my father. It was taken on New Guinea, before the New Britain landing.

In the picture my father has just been promoted to major, and he is standing like a major: helmet on his hip, wearing gloves, the .45 slung on his right hip, the binocular case on his left hip. It is an imperious pose; he is strutting his stuff. It's unlike any photograph I've ever seen. I've seen group pictures of officers on Guadalcanal that looked like class-reunion pictures in fatigues. I've seen the posed picture of my father on Pavuvu, and I've seen the formal photographic portraits that accompanied the newspaper clippings. I've seen the volleyball team, fourteen shirtless men, and I've seen the snapshots some of the men sent me from their visits to the farm—snapshots they had at the ready to send me, half a century after they'd been taken.

But this was the only picture I'd ever seen of the man as commanding officer. Faded into sepia, it nonetheless glowed. It was my father at his peak. It is my father the marine as I'd never seen him, and now knew him to have been.

"I want you to have it," Elmer Miller says, and while I protest, he reaches down and begins to peel it off the black construction-paper page. But it is tenacious. The glue is tough.

The next thing I know, Jack Parrish is at our side. He's produced a pocketknife and he's given it to Miller, who very gently cuts in beneath the photograph, gently lifts it off the page, and hands it to me.

• • •

The plane lifts off from the Las Vegas airstrip at midnight, heading east, and I am left alone in the dark to consider the heroes. I read George Hunt's book *Coral Comes High*.

"I had often asked some of them why they were fighting," Hunt wrote. " 'I don't know, exactly,' [one] replied. 'I do know that my father went through hell in the last war. He was gassed and still has to go to the hospital now and then to be treated. So I figured that if Dad, after going through what he did, would want his son to go through the same thing, there must be something in it.'

"It seems to me," George Hunt wrote, "that his answer conveyed the deep-rooted loyalty which can bind members of a family to each other, to their home and their way of life in their community. This and the pressure of maintaining one's self-respect and the respect of one's fellow men are the principal factors that motivate one to enlist, to fight, and to continue to fight, and possibly die."

The last time George Hadzidakis saw my father was at a reunion in New York.

" 'Forty-nine, maybe 'fifty. I'm standing on the street in New York, and all of a sudden there's this commotion. And the marines are marching down the street: 'Hip! Hip! Hip!' Four abreast, and your dad's in front. He says, 'Hadzidakis, get in here.' And we marched down to wherever we were going. It wasn't 'What a coincidence,' or 'Hey, look who's here.' It was 'Hadzidakis!' "

"A few years after the war, I'm coming home on the elevated train in Chicago," Bill Looney told me. "I've been to see my future wife. Early in the morning. I'm asleep in the subway car. A guy comes up and sits next to me and wakes me up and says, 'You're out awful late, lieutenant.' It was Tom. I couldn't believe it. I was so glad to see him."

The last time Looney saw my father was at lunch in New York. When Looney was working at the United ticket office in the East Side Airlines Terminal next to Grand Central, he and Jake Omdahl and my father and a half-dozen others who used to work in the city used to meet for a weekly lunch in the early fifties at an Irish place on Park and Forty-third.

Discussion of the war, Jake Omdahl recalls, never came up. When my father's plane crashed, the lunch club met and went out to Bronxville for the funeral as a group.

"I remember the last time I saw him," Eddie Bryan told me. "I was in the Third Marines at Camp Pendleton, on maneuvers. He came out to California."

It was 1959. He was looking for a location to build the Sacramento plant for Custom-Made Paper Bags.

"You know how big Pendleton is?" Bryan asked me. "He came right up on the base, found out where I was. I picked him up in a jeep and brought him up. We went out into a field. It was midnight. We drank a bottle of scotch. It was just like old times. That was the last time I saw him."

Eddie Bryan remembers finding out about my father's death in the newsletter of the First Marine Division, *The Old Breed News*.

"I still have it," he told me. "You think I would have saved that if I didn't think a lot of your father? We all did.

Your father was a great man. We would have followed him
to the gates of hell."

As far as I can tell, they did.

When I return from Las Vegas, there is a note in the mail
from Ray Fenton, on stationery that features a pen-and-ink
drawing of a mountain home in Montana. Ray's home.

The note includes a photograph of the volleyball team
on Pavuvu. By now, three or four men have sent me the
volleyball picture—have gone out to have it copied, or sent
me the original, feeling that it should be mine now—and I
call to thank him. I marvel at the consistency: each of them
able to put their hands on the photograph, each of them
keeping such perfect and permanent records of the old
days. By now, I have come to guard their notes and letters
and cards, and several times have thought back to the
cartons of letters from marines that I first discovered in
Washington, donated by an author after his research for
his book was done. I cannot understand how he could bear
to have sent them off.

We fall to talking about the marines, and the things I
have been thinking about. I ask Ray Fenton why each of
the men in the volleyball photograph—some lean, some
plump, some handsome, some homely, all bonded by having enlisted in the marines—I ask him why they fought.

"They were fighters—they loved the marine corps," Ray
Fenton tells me. "They weren't fighting for country. They
were fighting for their buddies, and for what they thought
the marines were.

"It was a very special advantage there, the Semper Fi
feeling. A different spirit. A different war. And a different

kind of people. No one took a vote on whether it was a good idea to go up the hill. We just did it.

"Now there's a lack of commitment, somehow. An irresponsibility to one another. That never was even a factor with us. Now there's a new definition of Semper Fi: 'I got mine, and look out for yourself.' "

I ask him what it used to mean.

"It was, 'We'll do it together. We will always be faithful to one another.' We were brothers. Took care of each other. There was a camaraderie, and your dad exemplified that. He did what was expected."

Ray Fenton tells me he'll never forgive me if I'm ever anywhere near him in Montana and don't drop in to visit.

"I play a pretty mean game of tennis," he says.

I allow as to how I'm not much of a tennis player.

"Well, I mix a pretty good gin martini," he says.

In that case, I tell him, he can count on me. I'll stand in for my father.